France à la carte

Richard Binns

Chiltern House

To
Anne,
Andrew and Sally Anne,
who have shared with me
so many of the pleasures
of France

© Richard Binns 1981 (Text and Maps).
First published 1981 by Chiltern House Publishers Limited, Chiltern House,
Amersham Road, Amersham, Bucks HP6 5PE.

ISBN 0 9507224 4 8

Illustrations reproduced with the permission of the French Government Tourist Office,
178 Piccadilly, London W1; and SNCF/Centre Audio-Visuel, 179 Piccadilly, London W1.

Editing assistance Jane Watson.
Maps by Richard Binns and H. Plews Gregory, Maulden, Beds.
Cover by Frank Clancy, Clan Creative Limited, 17 London End, Beaconsfield, Bucks.
Typeset by Art Photoset Limited, 64 London End, Beaconsfield, Bucks.
Printed by Butler & Tanner Ltd., Frome, Somerset.

INTRODUCTION

France à la carte is not a book about French cuisine or the country's wines and cheeses: nor does it describe any of France's splendid hotels and restaurants. (A second book of mine—*French Leave*—tries to do justice to some of those incomparable delights.) This book takes a look at the many hundreds of holiday attractions awaiting all visitors to that seductive country across the Channel. Those attractions are endless: they appeal to the young or the not-so-young, to the energetic or the not-so-energetic, to the sportsman, the outdoor enthusiast, the historian or the naturalist; indeed, to every type of visitor. My aim is to list them in a novel way, and I have included scores of maps to help you locate the many attractions—some of which are still largely *undiscovered.*

Many people will claim that they know a country (or a region within a country) quite well—after just passing through. How wrong they are: 99 per cent of tourists miss most of the real treasures and pleasures—both scenic and man-made—simply because they have not researched and discovered, beforehand, just what is hiding in the rural corners of the countryside.

Maps are the key. I count myself fortunate that I have used maps as thoroughly as I have used travel guides to discover where the pleasures of the countryside are hidden, both in my own islands and in many other parts of the world—but especially in France. Most guide books list where the great art and architectural wonders, created by our forefathers, can be found—and little more. But Nature has created her own marvels and they, too, like all art forms, can fire the imagination and stir the emotions just as strongly. Maps are the only certain way of showing readers just where they can find both the marvels of nature and of man. I have provided scores of small-scale maps to help you pinpoint those treasures: use large-scale maps for greater detail. I have never bought a map—either in the U.K. or in France—which has not returned a dividend many times over! The chapter—*A Day to Remember*—tries to capture the spirit of this book; do read it.

This book is for the motorist—in his own or a hired car. It does not pay too much attention to the great cities and it ignores Paris; motorists would be best advised to leave their cars at home when they visit that charming capital city. I know of no better guide book in the world than the Michelin Green Guide for Paris. Though the other 18 Green Guides do not match it, nevertheless, they are all very good; unhappily, only six of the 19 are in English.

Some brief notes to help you get the best from *France à la carte.* Use the regional index in addition to the general index: for example—if you are spending a few days in Burgundy the page numbers listed for that region will refer you to the many chapters describing its myriad attractions. If you want hotel or restaurant suggestions, use *French Leave* (the two books complement each other well—put together they fit like gloves), the *Logis de France* Guide (obtainable from the F.G.T.O.), or the Michelin Red Guide. My maps use the abbreviation *Mich* for Michelin; and indicate the number of the Michelin yellow maps that you should refer to for much greater detail. In turn, the yellow maps will allow you to refer to those places in the Red Guide where hotels and restaurants are located. All names shown in **bold** print in *France à la carte* are identified on the accompanying maps.

Make great use of the French Government Tourist Offices in your own country (see the list of some of these offices on page 144). In France, get used to asking for help at the *Syndicat d'Initiative* (Tourist Office) in each town or village. The simple objective of *France à la carte*—as it is with *French Leave*—is to give you many of the clues you need—supported perhaps by your own further research and your own discoveries—to enjoy the best pleasures of that superb country.

Good hunting—and enjoy France!

CONTENTS

A Day to Remember 7

Delights of the French Regions

Best of Brittany 9
Best of Burgundy 11
Detour through Brittany 13
Detour through Burgundy 15
Detour in the Dordogne 17
Detour in the Massif Central 19
Detour in Normandy 21
Hidden Corners of Auvergne 23
Hidden Corners of the Côte d'Azur 25
Hidden Corners in the Heart of France 27
Hidden Corners of the Loire 29
Hidden Corners of the North 31
Hidden Corners of Poitou-Charentes 33
Hidden Corners of Provence 35
Wine Country 37
Wine Villages & Towns 39

Historical Milestones Relived

Battlefields 41
Henry IV of Navarre 43
Journeys of Joan of Arc 45
Napoléon's Return 47
Roads to St-Jacques-de-Compostelle 49
William the Conqueror 51

Man-Made Marvels of France

Ancient Abbeys 53
Cathedrals 55
Châteaux Country 57
Fortified Towns 59
Hilltop Sights & Sites 61
Ports 63
Railways—State-owned 65
Railways—Privately-owned 67
Roman France 69
Shrines 71
Treasures of the Ile de France 73
Treasures of the Towns 75

A Mélange for the Arts, Sports and Outdoor Enthusiast

Artists 77
Beaches 79
Fishing 81
Golfing 83

Monte-Carlo Rally Country 85
Motoring Mementoes 87
Tour de France Highlights 89
Walking 90
Waterways 91

Pleasures of Nature

Etangs 93
Forests 95
Regional Nature Parks 97
Seasons 99
Spas 101

Scenic Splendours of France

Cirques 103
Coastlines—Atlantic 105
Coastlines—Mediterranean 107
Gorges—the Famous Ones 109
Gorges—the Unknown Ones 111
Grottoes & Caves 113
Islands 115
Lakes 117
Mountain-top Views 119
Roads that go Nowhere 121
Routes des Alpes 123
Routes des Pyrénées 125

Unknown Rivers of France

Bienne & Ain 126
Chapeauroux & Allier 127
Charentonne & Risle 128
Cure & Cousin 129
Dessoubre & Doubs 130
Indre 131
Loire 132
Nive 133
Truyère & Lot 134
Vézère 135

Regional Index 137

Index of Places 138

French Leave—Useful Addresses 144

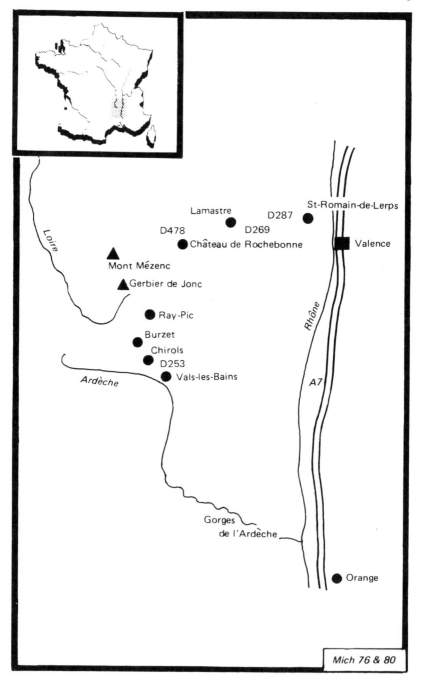

Mich 76 & 80

A DAY TO REMEMBER

Why is it that some hours of our life fix themselves so vividly in our memories? One of the special pleasures given to mankind is when the subconscious mind allows us to recall, years later, the joyful delights of sights and sounds from past moments in time—to be savoured whenever the human spirit needs refreshing.

For my wife and me, one example of this human heritage was a day we once spent in France during the last week of May. It was a day when Mother Nature was at her enchanted best; a fairyland of different colours, moods and scenes. Covering the same route two months earlier or later—though still worthwhile—undoubtedly would not have left the same crystal-sharp images in our minds; choosing the best season of the year was an important ingredient in creating that marvellous day.

Another essential ingredient—demonstrating most effectively the spirit of this book—was the use of large-scale maps. Nature often keeps her most alluring treasures to herself—maps alone help you to find them.

The direct route from **Orange** to **Valence** is 100 kilometres long. On the A7 that boring journey would take an hour of your time; our *day* took nine inspiring hours.

It started with skies full of black clouds; by 10 a.m. it was raining very heavily. Our initial objective had been to enjoy the spectacular D290 **Gorges de l'Ardèche** road; one that offers the chance to view some of France's best river and gorge scenery. Because of the downpour we made no stops; the 47 kilometres journey—it normally takes us three hours—was completed in little over an hour.

When we reached **Vals-les-Bains** it had stopped raining. Just before **Chirols**, on the narrow **D253**, we paused to enjoy both the views and our picnic lunch. Blue skies had appeared; the earlier wind and rain had left the air clear and bracing. Far below us lay the infant **Ardèche**; to the west serried ranks of hills.

We continued north to **Burzet**, where we stopped to gasp at the roaring, rushing river views; the earlier showers were now working for our benefit. Beyond Burzet the scenery unobtrusively changed. We were climbing towards the watershed between the Atlantic and the Mediterranean and this was reflected in the tints and shades of the woods and pastures. The **Ray-Pic** Cascade was superb—well worth the 15 minutes walk to admire its foaming fall down the mountainside.

The climb continued through mixed evergreen and deciduous woods to open meadows where, at a height of 1400 metres, we came upon the most breathtaking sight. The pastures were carpeted with wild flowers: sheets of wild daffodils and large yellow marsh buttercups, interlaced with huge splashes of purple violas. In the space of a few metres we saw six types of orchid hidden amongst the blankets of colour and we lost count of the number and variety of wild flowers. Within a few kilometres the *show* was to finish; we have not seen its like elsewhere in the Alps.

Reluctantly we carried on: first past the source of the **Loire**, then under the shadow of the **Gerbier de Jonc** and **Mont Mézenc**. Extensive views, made razor-sharp by the sparkling air, lay in all directions. We passed the **Château de Rochebonne (D478)** and two hours later we were in **Lamastre**. Rather than descend by the D534, we chose an alternative; the narrow lanes of the **D269** and **D287**.

At about 6 p.m. we stood at the observation tables above the village of **St-Romain-de-Lerps**. Below us and far to the east lay a glorious panorama, illuminated by the setting sun behind us. The views from the tables are illustrated by 38 hand-painted ceramic tiles; created 40 years ago, they helped us to pinpoint dozens of scenes, some 100 kilometres away. We tarried a long time at that quiet spot, chaperoned by an inquisitive herd of goats. Eventually we descended to the **Rhône** below, regretting the end of a *perfect day*. Good fortune had one more hand to play that evening; we enjoyed a memorable dinner. But that's another story!

8

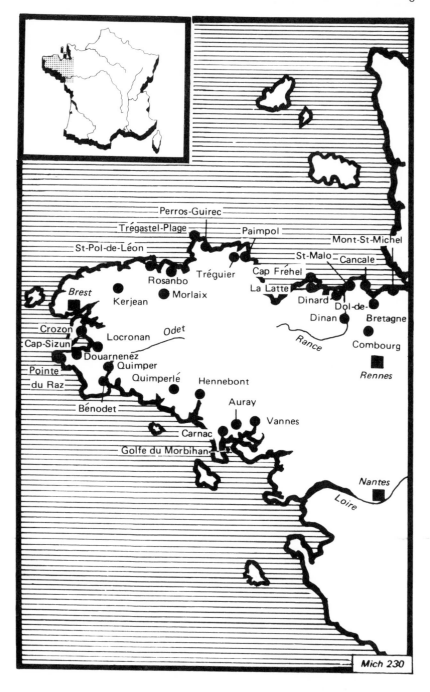

Perros-Guirec
Trégastel-Plage
Paimpol
St-Pol-de-Léon
Mont-St-Michel
St-Malo
Cancale
Rosanbo
Tréguier
Cap Fréhel
La Latte
Brest
Morlaix
Kerjean
Dinard
Dol-de-
Dinan
Bretagne
Crozon
Locronan
Odet
Combourg
Cap-Sizun
Rance
Douarnenez
Pointe
Quimper
Rennes
du Raz
Quimperlé
Hennebont
Bénodet
Auray
Carnac
Vannes
Golfe du Morbihan
Nantes
Loire

Mich 230

BEST OF BRITTANY

It is almost an impossible task to set down, on one page, the best sites, sights and treasures of this huge expanse of country—country so unlike the rest of France in its topography, its customs and in the character of its proud people; Celtic in origin, thinking and outlook.

It has been made a bit easier for me in that I have been able to include some of its delights—coasts, ports and beaches are examples—elsewhere in the book. What others, amongst so many that remain, can I beg you to seek out?

Start with the greatest of them all; the unique and spectacular **Mont-St-Michel**. Every step you take up the steep climb to the Romanesque and Gothic abbey will be rewarded a hundred times over by the breathtaking splendour of the buildings, the cloisters, the ramparts and the enthralling seaviews.

Nearby, at **Dol-de-Bretagne**, is the strangely named St-Samson's Cathedral, a 700 year old granite giant. At the port of **Cancale** are the famous oyster beds. From **St-Malo** take a trip up the River **Rance**—particularly if you have children with you. The excursion will include a visit to the nearby tidal power station. **Dinan** is my personal favourite—the loveliest of Breton towns: the gardens, the old streets, the splendid squares and the views from the Jardin Anglais (the inspiration of many painters) all blend together in a scintillating way to please any visitor.

Further inland is the small town of **Combourg**—its fortress-like castle with its great towers overlooks a lake. Inside the castle is a museum devoted to Châteaubriand who spent two years of his youth there.

Another fine boat trip is from **Dinard** to **Cap Fréhel**—as Michelin says 'worth a journey.' Fantastic cliffs, pounding surf and seas, hundreds of birds, extensive views and a lighthouse: no wonder my children got so excited by it all. To be frank, so did I! Don't bypass the nearby fort at **La Latte**.

Continuing westwards around the northern Brittany coast are a series of pleasant resorts; **Paimpol**, **Perros-Guirec** and **Trégastel-Plage**, amongst them. Two fine cathedrals grace the towns of **Tréguier** and **St-Pol-de-Léon**: St-Tugdual at Tréguier and the Ancienne Cathédrale at St-Pol. St-Pol is fortunate, too, to have the Chapelle du Kreisker with its magnificent belfry—a real eye-catching pleasure.

South-east of St-Pol is **Morlaix**—the town is built on steep hillsides and has many old streets and buildings; it is dominated by a huge railway viaduct. To the west is **Kerjean** with a fine château; to the east is another château at **Rosanbo**—a 14th century building with gardens by Lenôtre.

The southern coast of Brittany has its share of *essential* detours. The magnificent seaviews from the **Crozon** Peninsula, from the cliffs of the **Pointe du Raz** and the **Cap Sizun** Bird Sanctuary—a few kilometres to the east—are breathtaking, exciting and not-to-be-missed highlights for all visitors. **Douarnenez** (a flourishing Breton port), **Locronan** (with its dark granite houses, its church and the extensive views from the hills above the old town) and **Quimper** (the cathedral, the old town and the River **Odet**) all deserve to be explored and enjoyed.

Like the Rance in the north, the Odet provides many differing possibilities for boating trips. The excursion from Quimper to **Bénodet** is the best of them.

Continuing down the coast are two pleasant, small towns; **Quimperlé** and **Hennebont**. Both are handsome places and both have nice river country as an added bonus—to the south of Quimperlé are splendid forests.

Finally, to the south are the strange *megaliths* of **Carnac**—3000 of these granite pieces of all sizes and shapes are scattered over the ground. **Vannes**, an old historical town near the **Golfe du Morbihan**, deserves your attention—boat trips from Vannes and **Auray** are an exhilarating way of enjoying this *inland* sea.

10

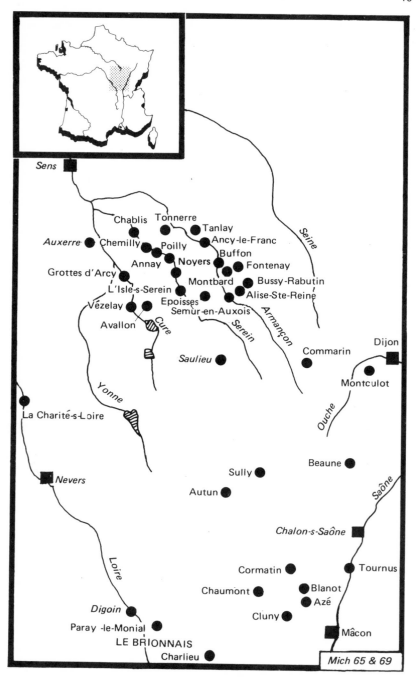

Mich 65 & 69

BEST OF BURGUNDY

There is one spot in Burgundy that I find perhaps the most inspiring place I know—**Vézelay**. I suppose it must be a combination of reasons why this is so: the sheer beauty and size of the great Basilica of Ste-Madeleine; the surrounding terraces with their enormous trees; and the views from the heights over the green Burgundian valleys lying under the hill. The sense of history past pulses strongly through your heart: Saint Bernard preached the Second Crusade here; Richard the Lionheart and Philippe-Auguste, arch-enemies, undertook jointly the Third Crusade from this spot; and Thomas à Becket took refuge here. The church was restored by our old friend Viollet-le-Duc over 100 years ago—there is no better example of his work anywhere in France. Please don't ignore this exquisite corner of rural France.

A circular tour, starting at **Avallon**, displays many of the glittering gems in the Burgundian crown of precious treasures. First, follow the **Serein** Valley, through **L'Isle-s-Serein**, the sleepy old towns of **Noyers, Annay, Poilly** and **Chemilly**, to **Chablis**, the home of marvellous dry white wines. Then go east to **Tonnere**—well worth exploring; detour to the Château de **Tanlay** and its intricate links with the Coligny brothers and memories of the Religious Wars in the 16th century. Further up the **Armançon** Valley is **Ancy-le-Franc**, a Renaissance castle with splendid rooms and tapestries. Continue south; don't miss the Forges de Buffon at **Buffon**, six kilometres before **Montbard**—an unusual *ancient monument*. Then comes Montbard itself—full of interest—and to the south-east is the best of all the châteaux of Burgundy: **Bussy-Rabutin**, a delightful, small building with lovely gardens, designed by another old friend of ours—Lenôtre. His name (and that of Viollet-le-Duc) appear often in this book.

Elsewhere I have written about the abbey at **Fontenay**, the Roman citadel of **Alise-Ste-Reine** and the fortified town of **Semur-en-Auxois**; all these are close to Montbard and all can be part of a one or two days' tour. Return to Avallon via **Epoisses**—renowned for its cheese, its old town and its fortified château.

Far to the south of Burgundy is a small hilly area called **Le Brionnais**: it sits on the eastern side of the Loire—**Paray-le-Monial** is on the northern edge, and **Charlieu** on the southern border. Both these towns are interesting places. Paray is one of the most important places of pilgrimage in France—the impetus to build the Sacré-Cœur in Paris came from this town. Its own Basilica of the Sacré-Cœur is a perfect example of Burgundian Romanesque architecture. Charlieu has its world famous Bénédictine abbey —the cloisters are especially delightful. Between these two towns are several villages each with their own fine example of Romanesque churches—all of them in green, wooded hills far from the rushing crowds.

Several other châteaux are dotted throughout the region and deserve your time if you are close at hand. West of **Mâcon** and **Tournus** are **Chaumont**—it has intriguing 17th century stables; and **Cormatin**—a Renaissance building and close to **Cluny**. West of **Dijon** is the 17th century château at **Commarin** with its own moat. South of the **Ouche** Valley is **Montculot**, once owned by Lamartine.

Amongst the natural attractions of Burgundy are three sets of caves: in the **Cure** Valley are the **Grottes d'Arcy** and further south, near Cluny, are the caves at **Azé** and **Blanot**. Both Azé and Arcy caves have water as a feature.

There are two spots which must be mentioned in this short chapter: firstly the château at **Sully**—a superb Renaissance building amidst a great park, midway between **Beaune** and **Autun**; and secondly the town of **La Charité-s-Loire**—its magnificent river setting, the ancient town with its glorious centrepiece of the Eglise Notre-Dame, all combining to make it one of the best of the many Loire marvels. Burgundy is full of treasures—explore it thoroughly and you will find dozens more. Out of season it is at its best—quiet and inspiring.

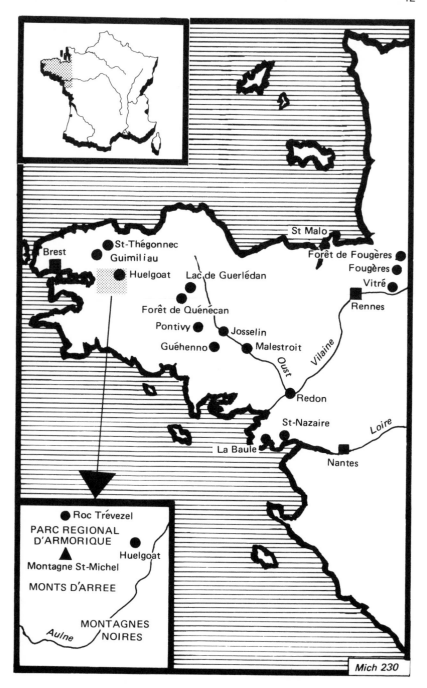

DETOUR THROUGH BRITTANY

Most visitors to France associate Brittany with its ports, its coastline, its cliffs, its sands and its world-famous towns, like **St-Malo**, **Brest**, **St-Nazaire** and **La Baule**; the first three are part of the great story of the sea.

But there is an inland Brittany, quiet, appealing and ignored by the masses. I promise you that the few days taken to cover the general route I describe here will be happy ones—covering different parts of the region as you move east.

Start in the area east of Brest—at **St-Thégonnec**, on the N12. Here, and at **Guimiliau**, are the best examples of the walled *enclos paroissiaux* (parish enclosures); calvaries, where scores of remarkable 400 year old sculptures fill the cemeteries and churchyards. You will not see anything like it elsewhere in France.

Bear south-east towards **Huelgoat**. This run will take you through the **Monts d'Arrée** and the **Armorique** Regional Nature Park—there are fine views from **Montagne St-Michel** and **Roc Trévezel**. Huelgoat and the surrounding country is my favourite part of inland Brittany (the *Argoat*). These enchanting hills are carpeted with forests of oak, spruce, pine and beech; scattered within them are huge blocks of granite and sandstone—there are many rock formations worth exploring. It is a paradise for walkers.

To the south of Huelgoat are the **Montagnes Noires**; lower than the Arrée hills to the north, they show a deserted and different face of the Breton countryside.

Changing the scene again, I suggest you now head due east to one of the best inland sights of Brittany—the glorious expanse of water called **Lac de Guerlédan**. Drive through the lanes that surround it; some of the country is wooded (the **Forêt de Quénécan**) and there are many fine natural sights, pretty viewpoints and charming ancient villages and hamlets to please you. All of it is enchanting walking terrain, full of broom and gorse in the spring and early summer.

Now follow part of the famous canal Napoléon built from Brest to **Nantes**—as far as **Pontivy**, a bustling, thriving market town. The next port of call is **Josselin**, alongside the River **Oust**. These waters reflect the towers and walls of the most picturesque castle in Brittany. Not far away is the small village of **Guéhenno** with a fine calvary.

Further down the canal are the towns of **Malestroit** and **Redon**. Malestroit is a small, old medieval town with interesting Renaissance and Gothic houses—many of them with intriguing, amusing sculptures on their façades. Redon, a bigger town, is at the junction of the canal and the River **Vilaine**; both waterways provide many river and canal cruising possibilities, discussed elsewhere in this book. The Church of St-Sauveur is its special highlight; a fine tower, cloister and interior are the attractions—all dating back 600 to 800 years.

Now aim north-east again towards **Rennes**. These days a series of new roads bypass the city. If you choose, you can do the same and continue to quieter attractions. However, the bypass roads, which are toll-free, have meant that most through-traffic ignores the city centre. Perhaps this reason alone would justify a diversion into the centre, where the old town, which is all that remains from the great fire of 1720, is full of interesting, ancient streets—all well worth exploring on foot. See the various museums and the Law Courts.

Continue east to the castle at **Vitré**. This is a superb example of preserved Brittany at its best. Its castle fascinated our youngsters a decade ago. **Fougères**, and the nearby State Forest, have in the past also greatly entertained our children. The towers, walls, keep and ramparts of the castle at Fougères are all perfect examples of the picture that youngsters must have in their minds of forts from ancient times. Now that our children are teenagers they wouldn't thank you for the chance to visit them again—10 years ago it was a different story.

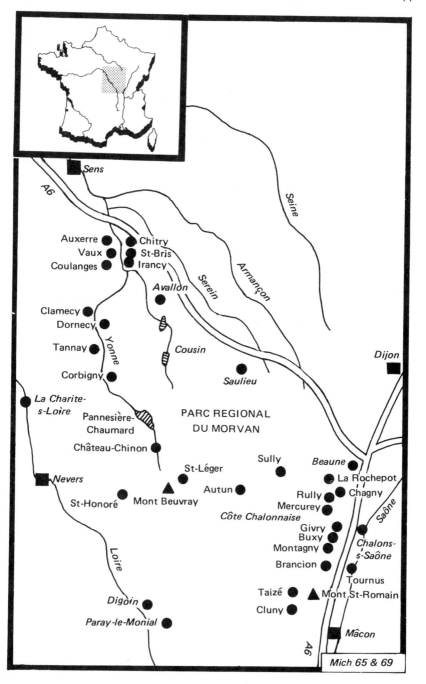

DETOUR THROUGH BURGUNDY

There are two ways of getting from **Auxerre**—in the north of Burgundy—to **Tournus**—in the south. One way would be to use the A6 Autoroute: it would take you about one or two hours I should think. The other route would take at least a day—I guarantee it will be the one you will remember for the rest of your life.

Auxerre is an ancient town with a famous Gothic cathedral, is full of lovely churches and has many historical stories to tell. Amongst them is the tale of how Marshal Ney and his Royalist forces joined up with Napoléon—as all the others had done, from the Côte d'Azur northwards, on his return to France. Follow the **Yonne** on the west bank through **Vaux**. On both banks of the river—**Coulanges** on your side and **Irancy**, **Chitry** and **St-Bris** on the east side—are villages famed for their white, red and rosé wines. Explore the fields and hills surrounding all these villages. The vinegrowers have worked very hard in recent years to establish their vineyards again; centuries ago their wines were renowned. Alexandre Dumas included the *Clos de la Chaînette* wine amongst the greatest of the French reds—honour indeed! One big bonus with all these *local* wines —red, rosé, white or sparkling—is that they will not break the bank. Try them and enjoy them all.

Follow the Yonne through **Clamecy** (a treasure-trove of ancient homes and streets), **Dornecy**, **Tannay** and **Corbigny**—all picturesque towns and full of old buildings. Good goat's milk cheeses abound hereabouts.

Now the road climbs alongside the Yonne up to the man-made lake at **Pannesière-Chaumard**. If you have the time, explore the narrow lanes encircling the whole lake. **Château-Chinon** rewards you with an exceptionally extensive panorama from Le Calvaire above the town; the town itself is an attractive place.

Continue south, driving deep into the woods and hills of the **Morvan** Regional Park; just before **St-Léger**, make the short, one-way only, diversion to the summit of **Mont Beuvray**—more marvellous views will be your reward.

If time permits, navigate yourself through the lanes to **St-Honoré**—an attractive spa town. You will not believe that so much lovely country can be ignored by so many for so long—be happy that you are not included amongst that number.

Back to the east again, to **Autun**. Under no circumstances should you pass it by. It was an old Roman town, once called the *sister of Rome* by Julius Caesar; its 800 year old Cathedral of Saint-Lazare is a special highlight. From Autun continue east, making a short detour to the handsome château at **Sully**. Its setting is particularly attractive; it has a fine front, many towers, a moat and a bridge—all surrounded by a pretty park. The interior cannot be visited.

Your next port of call should be the château at **La Rochepot**, with its shining, multi-coloured tiled roof. Now aim due south for **Cluny**. Pass through **Chagny** and the wine villages of the *Côte Chalonnaise*: **Rully**, **Mercurey** (a short detour to the west), **Givry**, **Buxy** and **Montagny**. Fine wines come from this area; thankfully, at prices far less severe than their northern cousins.

Spend time in the old town of Cluny with its inspiring ruins—it is described elsewhere in this book. Just north of Cluny is **Taizé** with its community, founded by Brother Roger in 1940, which has attracted thousands of people, of all nationalities and particularly youngsters, searching for a meaning to their lives.

Finally, navigate the lanes due east from Taizé to the summit of **Mont St-Romain**: the Jura, the Alps, the **Saône**—all are included in your views. Then through the village of **Brancion**—do stop and see its old buildings and its site—finishing at **Tournus**. The Eglise St-Philibert, with its two huge medieval towers, is a landmark for miles around. It is well worth exploring the old town, the birthplace of the portrait painter Jean Baptiste Greuze—born here in 1725.

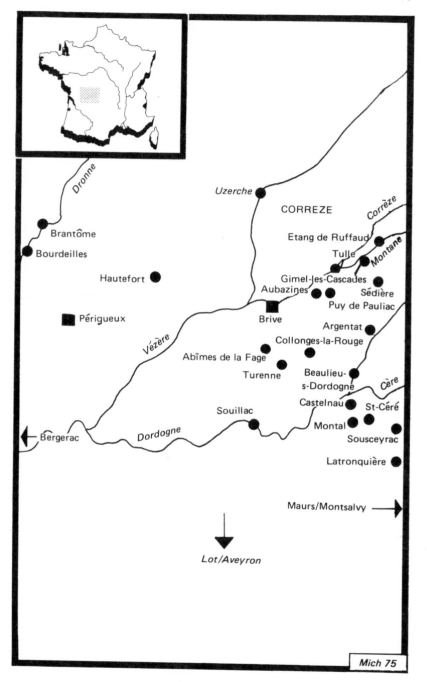

CORREZE

Uzerche

Corrèze

Etang de Ruffaud

Tulle

Montane

Gimel-les-Cascades

Aubazines

Sédière

Puy de Pauliac

Brive

Argentat

Collonges-la-Rouge

Abîmes de la Fage

Turenne

Beaulieu-s-Dordogne

Cère

Castelnau

St-Céré

Souillac

Montal

Sousceyrac

Bergerac

Dordogne

Latronquière

Maurs/Montsalvy

Lot/Aveyron

Dronne

Brantôme

Bourdeilles

Hautefort

Périgueux

Vézère

Mich 75

DETOUR IN THE DORDOGNE

Elsewhere in this book I describe some of the most famous treasures of the Dordogne country; most of those being alongside, or close to, the River **Dordogne**, between **Bergerac** and **Souillac**. This detour will encourage you to see other hidden parts of the Dordogne region, ignored by so many visitors.

Start at **Brantôme**—I fell in love with it over 20 years ago. The famous historian of the 16th century, Pierre de Bourdeille—the Abbé de Brantôme—brought fame to the abbey, and the town—which has an enchanting setting, made especially so by the River **Dronne**. His birthplace was in nearby **Bourdeilles**—its château, part Renaissance, part medieval, sits above the Dronne, downstream from Brantôme.

The fine town of **Perigueux** will attract you next—a cathedral, a museum and the old part of the town will particularly please you. Leave the town to the north-east and aim for the Château **Hautefort**, famous as the home of the troubadour Bertrand de Born, friend of Richard the Lionheart. It dominates the skyline and looks more like a Loire château than the fortress-like Dordogne examples.

The **Corrèze** Valley, north-east of Brive, has many pleasures awaiting the traveller prepared to make the effort to seek them out. **Aubazines** is a small, attractive village in wooded country—its ancient, 12th century Cistercian abbey is not to be missed. On the eastern side of the village, narrow lanes lead you to the summit of **Puy de Pauliac**, from where there are fine views of all the neighbouring country. Beyond **Tulle**, on the **Montane** (it flows into the Corrèze) is tiny **Gimel-les-Cascades**; you will be thrilled by the many waterfalls in this exciting river country. Seek out the **Etang de Ruffaud**, a small lake set amidst woods of pine, oak and birch. If you have the time search out the Renaissance château of **Sédière**—completely lost in superb country. Some of the best forests in France cloak the hills hereabouts.

Your next port of call is the country to the south-east of **Brive**; some of the finest hills in France lie in the *département* of **Corrèze**—it is totally unspoilt and its tiny and numerous lanes are as inviting as ever, many still *undiscovered.*

Point the car up as many of these lanes as possible. There are several sights you must not ignore. **Turenne**, an old village, is dominated by the ruins of a great castle. To the north-west, just before the N20, are the **Abîmes de la Fage**—underground caves full of fascinating stalagmites and stalactites. Find **Collonges-la-Rouge**; it is a unique place, where the houses and the church are built of red sandstone. It takes you back hundreds of years—you will want to linger there longer than time allows. Eventually, navigate over the hills to **Argentat**, on the banks of the Dordogne; it has a perfect river setting—seen at its best from the bridge.

Make a *deviation* to the north-east along the Dordogne if you must—but it is the run downstream, on the west bank, to **Beaulieu-s-Dordogne** I would prefer you to make. It is quiet, green and restful country. At Beaulieu is a Romanesque abbey.

Near the point where the River **Cère** joins the Dordogne, detour to the massive fortress of **Castelnau**, which has several perimeter walls and ramparts providing fine views of the two river valleys. Nearby, to the west of **St-Céré**, is a *pepper-pot* château at **Montal** (like the towers at Valençay in the Loire). Both these châteaux are amongst the best of all the Dordogne examples—don't miss them.

To finish this detour I implore you to drive up to the hills lying around **Sousceyrac**, **Latronquière**, **Maurs** and **Montsalvy**. The trees covering these hills are also amongst the best in France—particularly attractive in the spring or in the autumn, when their colours change. So many alternative pleasures await you—you can go south to the **Lot** and **Aveyron** valleys or further east into the Massif Central; one thing is certain, your last hours on this detour will be spent in lanes and villages ignored by the vast majority of travellers in France.

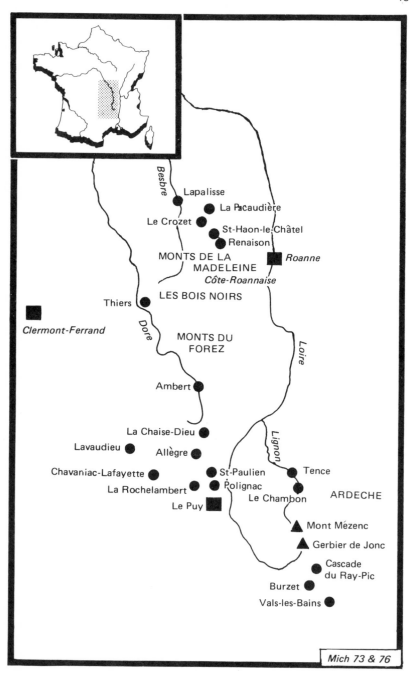

Besbre

Lapalisse

La Pacaudière

Le Crozet

St-Haon-le-Châtel

Renaison

MONTS DE LA MADELEINE

Roanne

Côte-Roannaise

LES BOIS NOIRS

Thiers

Clermont-Ferrand

Doré

MONTS DU FOREZ

Loire

Ambert

La Chaise-Dieu

Lavaudieu

Allègre

Lignon

Chavaniac-Lafayette

St-Paulien

Tence

La Rochelambert

Polignac

Le Puy

Le Chambon

ARDECHE

Mont Mézenc

Gerbier de Jonc

Cascade du Ray-Pic

Burzet

Vals-les-Bains

Mich 73 & 76

DETOUR IN THE MASSIF CENTRAL

I suggest you start this *deviation* at **Vals-les-Bains**, a small riverside spa in the **Ardèche** countryside. Be warned before you start: at every turn you will have an excuse to stop, stare and soak in the scenic pleasures made by man centuries ago, and those carved and painted by Mother Nature in such attractive ways. Take your time and navigate your way carefully through the myriad lanes.

First stop in **Burzet**—a tiny place with fine river views. Then north to seek out the source of the **Loire** at **Gerbier de Jonc**—the views from the 1551 metres high summit are very extensive. On your way there from Burzet do the *Monte* stage via the **Cascade** (Waterfall) **du Ray-Pic** (see *Monte-Carlo Rally Country*—page 85).

Immediately to the north of the Gerbier de Jonc is **Mont Mézenc**—higher by 202 metres. This mass of mountains is the watershed between the rivers that flow north to the Atlantic and those flowing south to the Mediterranean. Use all the lanes encircling Mont Mézenc: if you feel energetic enough it is not too long a walk to its summit, where you will be rewarded with the best views in the Ardèche. Please also read the chapter called *A Day to Remember* on page 7—where I describe this countryside more fully.

The **Lignon** Valley is super country—at its best in the autumn—particularly the stretch from **Le Chambon** to **Tence**. From Tence aim west to **Le Puy**; the strangest and most unusual of all the towns in France. I write about it elsewhere but, to remind you once again, it is surrounded by sharp, needle-like volcanic hills, some of them with chapels and statues on their summits.

If you have the time, make a short *deviation* westwards to the chateau at **Chavaniac-Lafayette**; the Marquis de Lafayette, a hero of the American War of Independence, was born there. See nearby **Lavaudieu** with its Bénédictine church and the ruins of the ancient abbey. (These two villages could well be visited after passing through **Allègre**—see the next paragraph; returning to rejoin the route at **La Chaise-Dieu**.)

You must now do some careful navigation. Immediately north of Le Puy is **Polignac** with its fortress home on a massive slab of granite. Just west of **St-Paulien** and its lovely church (itself 14 kilometres north of Le Puy—on the D906) is **La Rochelambert**, its romantic château full of memories of George Sand. Then up the D13 to **Allègre** which has a ruined castle and offers a fine panorama on all sides. Finally, at **La Chaise-Dieu** there is a great abbey which overshadows the tiny village; it is famous for its frescoes (one of the *Dance Macabre*) and its tapestries.

North now to the bustling market town of **Ambert** and the **Dore** Valley. Continue downstream for 30 kilometres but, at the point where the river goes west away from the main road, turn off to the right into the **Monts du Forez**. This 45 kilometres long strip of granite mountains is probably unknown by most Frenchmen, let alone foreigners. It is wooded, full of small villages, fields and valleys and offers utter seclusion.

As an alternative to seeing some of the Dore Valley, enter the southern end of these hills at Ambert—and then drive their entire length to **Thiers**. Either way that is where I suggest you finish this part of the detour; it has a marvellous situation, is full of old houses and is ignored by everyone—simply because it lies on an east–west route that is never used by English, Dutch or Belgian visitors.

To finish this detour through the Massif Central, I suggest you put aside some hours to explore all the hill country to the north of Thiers, called **Les Bois Noirs**: that name comes from its dark, sombre pine woods. It is full of fine views, some of which are across the **Besbre** Valley to a second set of hills—the **Monts de la Madeleine**. Seek out several old villages on the eastern slopes of these deserted hills: **La Pacaudière**, **La Crozet** and **St-Haon-le-Châtel** are amongst them. From **Renaison** come some fine, unknown wines: especially good are the rosé and the *Côte-Roannaise* reds (these go really well with Charolais beef). Make **Lapalisse** your final destination.

20

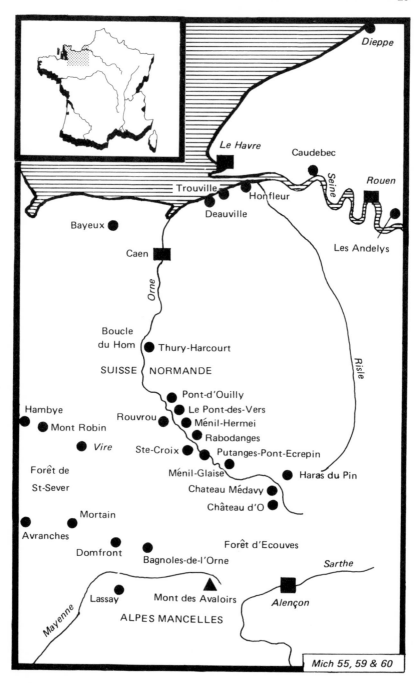

DETOUR IN NORMANDY

If you can choose any particular part of the year to make this detour, make it May, when Normandy's great apple orchards are laden down with blossom, destined to become that strong and fiery apple brandy, Calvados. As a bonus, its fields are full of wild, yellow irises and its woods, in the hills to the south, are at their best with their new mantle of green. It is all dazzling country.

Start in the south-west corner at **Avranches**; General Patton began his great attack across France here in August 1944—a monument commemorates that bit of history. Centuries earlier, Henry II made public penance in Avranches for the murder of Thomas à Becket in Canterbury Cathedral. At the square called La Plate-forme is the paving stone on which Henry II kneeled—barefooted and dressed only in a shirt.

From Avranches drive north to **Hambye** Abbey; a magnificent place, now in ruins, and dating from the 12th century. Nearby is **Mont Robin**; on clear days the view takes in the Channel Islands far to the west. Then south-east through the **Forêt de St-Sever** and pretty country to **Mortain**, which was destroyed during the war but attractively rebuilt—it has a particularly nice setting. **Domfront** has an impressive site; don't miss the extensive views from the ruined keep.

Continue to **Bagnoles-de-l'Orne**. It is one of the premier spa towns of France and is surrounded by woods and forests; especially attractive are the lake and river running through the town. Don't bypass the château at nearby **Lassay**.

Head south-east—to the small area between the **Mayenne** and **Sarthe** Rivers—it has the unlikely name of the **Alpes Mancelles**. It is true, together with the next port of call, that this is the highest ground in Western France; **Mont des Avaloirs**, at 417 metres, provides the best panorama. These *Alps* are nothing like the high mountains in Savoie—far to the south-east, on the border with Switzerland.

Now due north to the **Forêt d'Ecouves**—another of the great French forests—full of beeches, oaks, pines and spruce trees. Its highest point is also 417 metres. Continue north via the **Château d'O** and **Château Médavy** to **Haras du Pin**. A visit here—particularly for children—is a memorable event; it is the site of the Le Pin Stud, where 100 or so magnificent stallions are stabled; all of it set in a wooded park and with a handsome château as an added attraction.

Your next objective is to follow, as closely as you can, the lanes on either side of the River **Orne** as it flows due north to the sea. Start at **Ménil-Glaise**, then on through **Putanges-Pont-Ecrepin**, **Ste-Croix**, **Rabodanges**, **Ménil-Hermei**, **Rouvrou**, **Le Pont-des-Vers** to **Pont-d'Ouilly**. All this delightful country is called the **Suisse Normande**—it is hardly that, but, in its own special way, it is highly scenic and attractive. Years ago our children spent happy hours in the fields alongside the river banks. It was a vivid reminder that children are not always exclusively entertained by beaches and the sea. They made friends with a local farmer who allowed them to help with several tasks on his farm, including milking the cows. Those two days spent in that wooded river country left us all with happy memories.

Continue north to **Thury-Harcourt**. There make the short deviation to the **Boucle du Hom**—where the river makes a famous and unusual *loop*. Don't miss it.

At Thury various options are now open to you: **Caen**, **Bayeux** and the D-Day coast are directly ahead; to the north-east are the resorts of **Deauville** and **Trouville** and the attractive harbour at **Honfleur**. An alternative is to drive due east and link up with the run in the chapter called *Charentonne & Risle* (page 128).

Take each of them in their turn from west to east: but ensure you finish your detour by seeing as much of the **Seine** Valley as possible, starting at **Caudebec** and finishing at **Les Andelys**, where the formidable, ruined fortress Château-Gaillard, once the home of Richard the Lionheart, towers above the town and river!

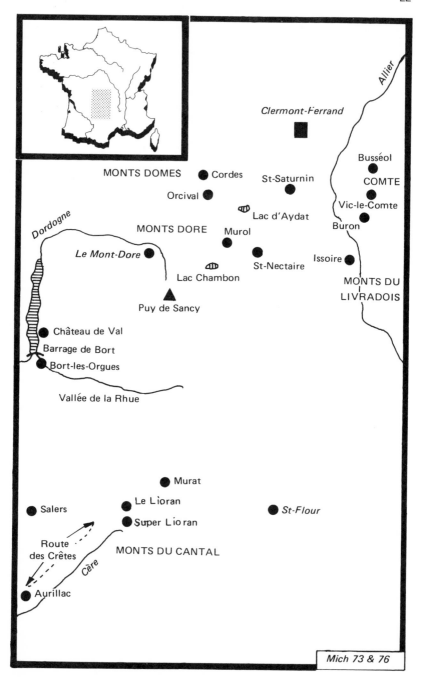

Clermont-Ferrand

Alliér

Busséol

MONTS DOMES   Cordes

St-Saturnin

COMTE

Orcival

Vic-le-Comte

Lac d'Aydat

Dordogne

MONTS DORE   Murol

Buron

Le Mont-Dore

Issoire

Lac Chambon   St-Nectaire

MONTS DU
LIVRADOIS

Puy de Sancy

Château de Val

Barrage de Bort

Bort-les-Orgues

Vallée de la Rhue

Murat

Salers

Le Lioran

St-Flour

Super Lioran

Route
des Crêtes   MONTS DU CANTAL

Cère

Aurillac

Mich 73 & 76

HIDDEN CORNERS OF AUVERGNE

There is no other area in France that rewards the traveller—prepared to make the effort to find them—with so many *hidden corners*; they appear at every turn.

My contribution towards encouraging you to seek out some of those lovely, secret places is to list for you a few that lie in the western half of the Auvergne. The chapter called *Detour in the Massif Central* (page 19) lists many of the quietest and best parts of the eastern half of Auvergne.

Start at **Murat** and aim for **Le Lioran** and **Super-Lioran**, high above it. Invigorating woods and views of the **Monts du Cantal** will reward you on this first part of your journey. Then make the long run down the **Cère** Valley—full of old villages and fine river scenes. At **Aurillac**, double back and use the **Route des Crêtes**—renowned for its fine views, particularly those to the east.

You should next aim for **Salers**—marvellously situated, high in the mountains and full of old houses. From Salers, **Bort-les-Orgues** is your next port of call. Approach it from the east along the **Vallée de la Rhue**. At Bort are strange organ-pipe rock formations; it is River **Dordogne** country and to the north is one of the most scenic of the many man-made lakes on the river. The **Château de Val**, on the eastern bank, is perhaps one of the most photographed in France; you will undoubtedly have seen it on many a tourist brochure or poster. The other man-made marvel is the **Barrage de Bort**—a high dam and an important hydro-electric power source.

To the north-east, a series of choices awaits you. The **Puy de Sancy** (make an excursion to the top in the cable-car) is the highest in the Massif Central at 1885 metres. To the east is **Lac Chambon**, **Murol** and **St-Nectaire**. The latter two villages are famous, rightly so, for their superb cheeses. St-Nectaire has the most perfectly proportioned Romanesque church in France—an exquisite building—and complemented by an enchanted setting. Murol has a ruined castle sitting on its own steep-sided hill which is a landmark for miles; by far the most interesting prospect of the ruin is to climb the D5 to the north and then see it, eagle-like, from above—a strange, frightening and forbidding sight.

Continue through the narrow roads to the **Lac d'Aydat**. Auvergne is at its best in spring or in autumn. I have seen the meadows in May full of wild flowers: narcissi, celandines, cowslips, wild daffodils, snowdrops and violets; in the autumn it is the turn of the lilac-shaded crocus, tiny dianthus and spiraea.

Before finishing your journey through this volcanic centre of France with a visit to two of its best treasures—described in the penultimate paragraph—various alternatives lie to your immediate east, adjacent to the River **Allier**. **St-Saturnin** is a splendid old village with a handsome Romanesque church, fountains and old houses. **Issoire** is a town and its special attraction is the Eglise St-Austremoine, a splendid Romanesque church built in the 12th century.

Immediately to the east of the Allier is some lovely hill country—deserted and ignored by everyone. It is called **Comté** and **Vic-le-Comte** is in its centre. From the two châteaux at **Buron** (to the south of Vic) and **Busséol** (to the north) you get extensive views of all the surrounding country, including the mountain ranges called **Dore**, **Dômes** (both to the west), **Comté** and **Livradois** (to the south-east).

The two final rich treasures that you must not pass by are the delightful château at **Cordes**, near Orcival, and the exquisite church in the village of **Orcival**—both special favourites of mine. The château, built in the 15th century, has been restored and has gardens by Lenôtre—a name which appears many times in these pages.

It really is superb country. I can hardly do justice to it. What you should do is to take your car up as many of the lanes as you can and, dead-ends or not, you cannot fail to revel in such invigorating, verdant mountain seclusion.

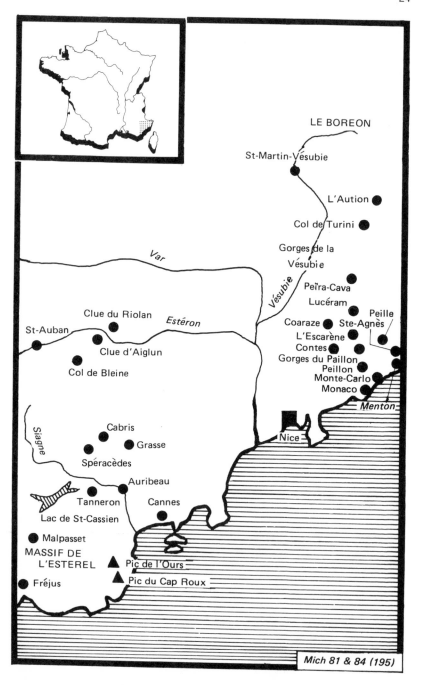

LE BOREON

St-Martin-Vésubie

L'Aution

Col de Turini

Gorges de la
Vésubie

Var

Vésubie

Peïra-Cava

Lucéram

Clue du Riolan

Estéron

Peille

Coaraze

Ste-Agnès

St-Auban

L'Escarène

Clue d'Aiglun

Contes

Col de Bleine

Gorges du Paillon

Peillon

Monte-Carlo

Monaco

Menton

Siagne

Cabris

Grasse

Nice

Spéracèdes

Auribeau

Tanneron

Cannes

Lac de St-Cassien

Malpasset

MASSIF DE
L'ESTEREL

Pic de l'Ours

Fréjus

Pic du Cap Roux

Mich 81 & 84 (195)

HIDDEN CORNERS OF THE COTE D'AZUR

I remember talking, some years ago, to two couples, one Dutch and one English, both of whom had bought their own villas on the Côte d'Azur and holidayed there each year for decades. They thought they knew the area well but were astonished to learn of *hidden corners*. They had never bothered to look at the local maps and presumably they had missed many of life's pleasures as a result. Don't make the same mistake. I love **Grasse**, **Cannes**, the flower market at **Nice**, **Monte-Carlo** and **Monaco**—but they alone are not exclusively the Coast! Countless other pleasures lie inland.

I want you to start in the wooded mountains of the red, craggy **Massif de l'Esterel**. Drive up the narrow forest tracks; if you are particularly energetic do the walks up to the **Pic de l'Ours** and the **Pic du Cap Roux**—most of the Côte d'Azur lies within your perspective—east, west and north.

Now go north to the **Lac de St-Cassien**, a man-made lake. The infamous **Malpasset** dam was to the south-west of this new lake; you may even have seen, from the A8, the huge blocks of concrete, from the broken dam, tossed down the valley by the tidal wave (hundreds lost their lives at **Fréjus**). Take the narrow lanes east through **Tanneron** and aim for **Auribeau**. (In February this is golden mimosa country.)

Auribeau, above the River **Siagne**, is the perfect, small, *perched* hill-top village. I promise you—you will want to return to it often.

Continue north to **Spéracèdes** and **Cabris**; you will pass, and stop at, countless small villas with terraces and walls covered in sheets of colour—oleander, bougainvilia, veronica and hibiscus. In May and June it is magical country. Your objective is the **Col de Bleine**, on the northern edge of Michelin map 84.

To the south of the Col you have been driving in Mediterranean scenery; at the summit and to the north are Alpine vistas. It is a cool, secluded and wooded spot and, incidentally, yet another famous Monte-Carlo Rally stage. In spring the valley floors are a sea of wild flowers; May is a marvellous month in any mountain area.

Make the short detour west to **St-Auban** to see the village and its famous gorge. But then double back to the **Estéron** Valley to gasp at the fabulous rift at Aiglun (**Clue d'Aiglun**) and within a short drive, the equally astonishing rift at Riolan (**Clue du Riolan**). Few people find their way to these wonders of nature.

That should be enough for one day—further chapters tell you about the merits of other sights in the **Var** area. Put aside a second day for the next suggestions.

Start with the **Gorges de la Vésubie**—where the **Vésubie** joins the Var. Drive north-east along the valley—first on one side, then the other—to **St-Martin-Vésubie**. To the north is **Le Boréon**; dead-end valleys enticing you to waterfalls, lakes, woods and perfect solitude. You are in the Mercantour Hunt Reserve; with luck you will see chamois, marmots and other wild animals in those protected hills.

Retrace your steps and climb the exciting **Col de Turini**—rallyists on the *Monte* cover this stage—in differing permutations—several times in the space of a few hours. Make the climb on the D68 to the panorama from **L'Aution**. South through the pines to **Peïra-Cava**, built precariously on a small rocky outcrop. Then **Lucéram** and west to **Coaraze**—a favourite *perched* village of mine—now much restored.

Finish your day of surprises by following the road through **Contes** to **L'Escarène**. South of the town are the **Paillon** gorges: make the sharp ascent—and detour—to **Peillon** (another delightful *perched* village) and finish by driving through **Peille** and **Ste-Agnès** (extensive views of the coast).

When you have enjoyed all that, ask any of your friends who know the area whether they have been excited by the sights as you will have been. I bet not one of them will know what you are talking about—but don't be too smug, as you still have dozens of other *hidden corners* to explore yourself on the Côte d'Azur!

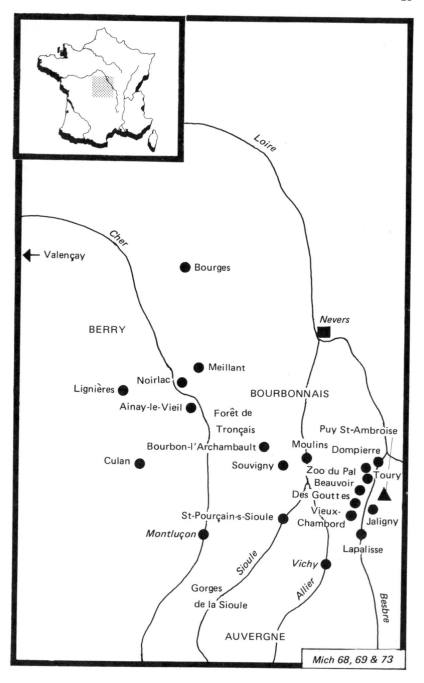

Mich 68, 69 & 73

HIDDEN CORNERS IN THE HEART OF FRANCE

My definition of the *Heart of France* is the regions known as **Berry** and **Bourbonnais**. I stray south of the latter to include a small section of the most northerly parts of **Auvergne** which, officially, stretches from Moulins to Le Puy.

Few tourists go out of their way to find the best of this expanse of countryside. Berry is flat, unexciting country—the plentiful wheat fields of France. Further south are gentler rolling hills. Everywhere meadows are green, the cattle graze contentedly, the poultry are plump: it is no wonder the country folk love their land and the generous harvests it provides. This is the true heart and soul of France—here, you sense, is where the basic strengths of France lie.

An excellent introduction to the area is to start at **Valençay**—this is in Berry territory, though most people consider it as Loire country. The château towers look just like *pepper-pots*—it is a favourite of ours and our children's; a park with animals appealed to them—the town to us.

Bourges is hardly *hidden*, but as so few people pass through this superb town, it may just as well be! It is full of old streets, houses, buildings and parks—it is one of the very best examples of France's medieval past. Its greatest treasures are the majestic Cathédrale St-Etienne and the Palais Jacques-Coeur with its richly decorated interior and elegant exterior. Don't bypass this largish town.

After absorbing the rich and inspiring treasures of Bourges, aim due south towards the **Cher**. At **Meillant** is the best of the Berry château—Italian in style. This is hardly surprising as both Meillant and Chaumont (on the Loire) were completed by Charles II of Amboise, one-time Governor of Milan.

To the south-west are four attractions worth seeking out. At **Ainay-le-Vieil** is a château with medieval ramparts and Renaissance buildings. At **Noirlac** is the Ancienne Abbaye de Noirlac, founded by St-Bernard in the 12th century. **Lignières** was where Calvin held many of his meetings in his student days at Bourges—today it is famous for its château. To the south is the inspiring, medieval fortress at **Culan**—Joan of Arc stayed there after Orléans had been captured by the French.

Now bear due east; don't miss the **Forêt de Tronçais**, written about elsewhere. **Bourbon-l'Archambault** is an enchanting small spa; between it and Moulins is **Souvigny** with its ancient Priory of St-Pierre. Its special treasure is its 12th century *calendrier*—an unusual sculpture showing scenes from the Zodiac.

Moulins is one of my favourite French provincial towns. Its tree-lined streets, the cathedral, and especially its clock tower—the Jacquemart—should not be missed. The latter will fascinate children. Every 15 minutes a family of four mechanical bell ringers use their hammers to tell the world the time: Jacquemart, Jacquette his wife, and their children Jacquelin and Jacqueline!

To the south are the pleasures of the small town of **St-Pourçain-s-Sioule** (building a fine reputation for its wines—the match of many of the famous Loire vintages) and to the south-west the impressive **Gorges de la Sioule**.

Due east from St-Pourçain-s-Sioule is the little-known **Besbre** Valley. I have already suggested you see that river in its infant stage as it descends from Les Bois Noirs to **Lapalisse**; many villages to the east of the Besbre are worth exploring (see *Detour in the Massif Central*—page 19).

But the Besbre, north from Lapalisse to **Dompierre-s-Besbre**, where it joins the **Loire**, has several charming little pleasures of its own. There are four notable châteaux: at **Vieux-Chambord**; **Jaligny**; **Beauvoir** and at **Toury**. From the **Puy St-Ambroise** you get a fine panorama of this northern section of the Besbre Valley. Near Dompierre is the small **Zoo du Pal**—guaranteed to keep the children happy. A pleasure park at **Des Gouttes** is also certain to do just the same.

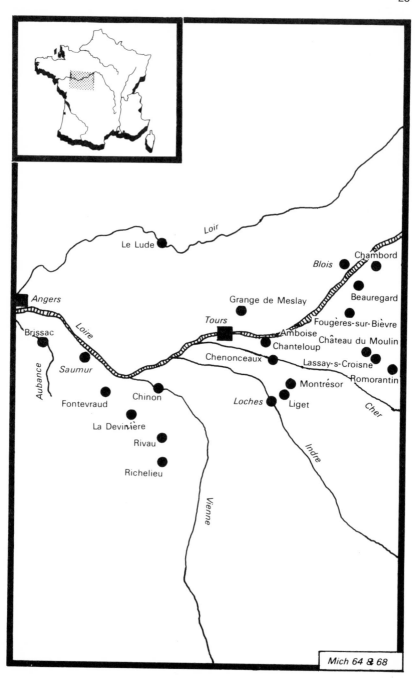

Loir

Le Lude

Blois Chambord

Grange de Meslay Beauregard

Angers Fougères-sur-Bièvre

Loire *Tours* Amboise Château du Moulin

Brissac Chanteloup

Aubance *Saumur* Chenonceaux Lassay-s-Croisne

Romorantin

Fontevraud Chinon Montrésor

Loches Liget Cher

La Devinière

Rivau

Richelieu Indre

Vienne

Mich 64 & 68

HIDDEN CORNERS OF THE LOIRE

Elsewhere I write about the world-famous attractions of the **Loire**. But here I am going to point you in the direction of some not so well-known treasures. Take the time and trouble to search them out—you may well have some to yourself.

Le Lude is an interesting enough Renaissance château but the real and only reason for visiting the town is to immerse yourself in the greatest of all the *son et lumière* spectacles. You watch this breathtaking show—given by over 300 people—from the opposite bank of the **Loir**. It is a real three star special.

From the terraces of the château at **Amboise**, with its lovely views of the Loire, you will also see, just 300 or 400 metres to the south-east, the rooftop of the simple Clos Lucé; the last home of Leonardo da Vinci. Visit the famous château, but don't miss this modest place—it is full of interest and contains fascinating examples of the work of this genius of a man. Other aspects of the history of Clos Lucé and its many personalities through the centuries are well presented.

It was Raymond Mortimer who first gave me the clue to the **Chanteloup** Pagoda. It sits just two kilometres south of Amboise; it is 144 feet high and is built in seven tiers. Find it, climb it, and enjoy fine views to east and west.

When you have seen **Chambord** and **Chenonceaux**, then make the navigating effort to find the simple, feudal château at **Fougères-sur-Bièvre**. The contrast is amazing.

Beauregard is worth a visit just to see the 363 historical portraits in the long picture gallery of the Renaissance château. They portray many of the great and important personalities of those history-filled centuries: Rabelais; Henry III of France; Henry VIII of England; Medici and Richelieu are amongst them. The floor of the gallery has another special treasure; Delft tiles telling the story of an army on the march in the time of Louis XIII.

The magnificent abbey at **Fontevraud** has several historical attractions. Its church contains the tombs of Henry II, Eleanor of Aquitaine (who died at Fontevraud in 1204), and their son, Richard the Lionheart. The octagonal Romanesque kitchen is astonishing: you will gasp at the ingenuity of its medieval builders.

Again, make the navigational effort to find the hamlet of **La Devinière** where Rabelais was born and spent his early childhood. The local manor house has a museum illustrating much of his life and work.

The Château **Brissac** has a fine site with a lovely park as a backdrop—the River **Aubance** flows through it. The building is an intriguing mixture of château and fort—it is privately-owned and it is renowned for its rosé and sweet white wines.

The **Grange de Meslay** is between the N10 and A10 Autoroute, just 9 kilometres north-east of Tours. The tithe barn is magnificent—built 700 years ago—and is a salutary reminder that our ancestors were skilled people indeed. Very few modern structures, built of stone and timber, can match its handsome grandeur.

The town of **Richelieu** is said to be one of the first *planned* towns in France. It was Cardinal Richelieu who organised it all in the 17th century.

Rivau is between **Chinon** and Richelieu; one of many local sights written about by Rabelais in *Gargantua*. It has a splendid château, now owned by the painter, Pierre-Laurent Brenot—some of whose paintings are on show here.

Montrésor is an attractive village and has a picturesque château alongside the River Indrois. The old church equals the château in both interest and charm. Just west of the village is the Chartreuse du **Liget**—a Carthusian monastery built by Henry II to make amends for the murder of Thomas à Becket.

Lassay-s-Croisne is lost in the depths of the Sologne (see page 93)—west of **Romorantin**. Near the village is the picturesque **Château du Moulin**, with its own moat. There is no better example to illustrate the words *Hidden Loire*.

30

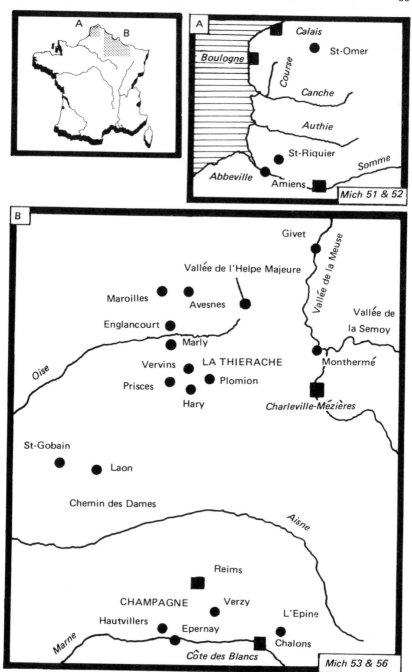

HIDDEN CORNERS OF THE NORTH

It is impossible to link one particular route across the entire width of northern France which will take you off the beaten track. What I am doing is to highlight specific areas —each of which can be explored en route to a final destination elsewhere in France, or during a weekend break.

Amiens will be known by all visitors to northern France. But how many travellers will have taken the trouble to find the strange *hortillonnages* of Amiens (water-gardens), cultivated by gardeners who move about their bits of marshy land in gondola-like boats? They and their forefathers have been there for centuries.

The **Somme** Valley—east and west of Amiens—is full of pools and meres; a paradise for fishermen and birdwatchers. To the north (detour via the church at **St-Riquier**) are three tiny valleys: the **Authie**, the **Canche** and the **Course**—all ignored by the speeding motorists, hell-bent on breaking their necks to either get to, or from, the Channel ports. It is fine, green, pastoral country.

Equally most people dash through **St-Omer**—this is a perfect example of a town and a region keeping its best attractions closely to itself. Next time you are that way—stop, park and explore on foot the real town to the east of the N43. You will be delightfully surprised at the elegant houses and the proud streets it contains. Don't judge the town by what you see from the N43!

The countryside surrounding **Avesnes** is famous for its cheeses and not much else; a pity, because a happy day or two can be spent at one of the many fine hotels in the vicinity, set in peaceful country. The **Vallée de l' Helpe Majeure**, to the east of Avesnes, is full of scenic interest: woods, lakes and small villages. **Maroilles**, west of Avesnes, is renowned for its cheese—and a 200 year old watermill.

La Thiérache is an area found to the south of Avesnes, on either bank of the **Oise** and south to **Vervins**. Here you can see several dozen fortified churches, built of brick with multi-coloured patterns in their walls. Amongst them are **Marly** and **Englancourt** —both near the Oise; south of Vervins are **Plomion**, **Hary** and **Prisces**. Search out at least one or two of them.

Further east, on the borders with Belgium, is the **Vallée de la Meuse**. This is ignored by most Anglo-Saxons as it lies near roads that *go nowhere*. Explore it from **Givet**, on the border, down to **Monthermé**: include the **Vallée de la Semoy** that joins it at this point. Fine river views; dark, dense woods; high hills; spectacular rock cliffs; all combine to make it a rewarding detour.

North-west of **Reims** is **Laon**, sitting on its high hill; a fine cathedral, in an equally fine setting, adds extra splendour to the exciting views from the ramparts and cliff-side promenades. Nearby is the forest of **St-Gobain**; in those appealing woods are several attractions, particularly two ancient abbeys.

Between Laon and Reims is a famous road running along the top of the hills between the River **Aisne** and a stream called the Ailette—the **Chemin des Dames**. Bitter fighting took place on these ridges during the First World War. Visit some of the many cemeteries and memorials and particularly spare time to see the Caverne du Dragon— a museum, set in a cavern, devoted to those bloody battles.

South of Reims are the hills of **Champagne** country. Visit the cellars of the famous firms at either Reims or **Epernay** (Moët & Chandon have a cellar there 25 kilometres long). The abbey at **Hautvillers**, just across the river from Epernay, is where the blind Dom Pérignon discovered how to put the bubbles into champagne, and keep them there! Before leaving the area to the north of the **Marne**, seek out the centuries old beech forest of **Verzy**: then explore the Marne Valley and the vineyards to the south of the river—the *Côte des Blancs*. Your final detour should be to the splendid 15th century Gothic church at **L'Epine**, east of **Chalons**.

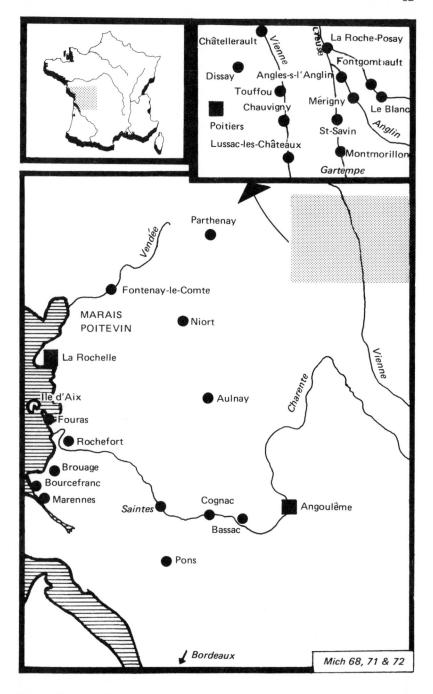

Châtellerault
Vienne
Creuse
La Roche-Posay
Fontgombault
Dissay
Angles-s-l'Anglin
Touffou
Mérigny
Le Blanc
Chauvigny
Anglin
Poitiers
St-Savin
Lussac-les-Châteaux
Montmorillon
Gartempe

Parthenay
Vendée
Fontenay-le-Comte
MARAIS
POITEVIN
Niort
La Rochelle
Charente
Vienne
Ile d'Aix
Aulnay
Fouras
Rochefort
Brouage
Bourcefranc
Marennes
Saintes
Cognac
Angoulême
Bassac
Pons

Bordeaux

Mich 68, 71 & 72

Many of my readers will have explored the fine towns of **Poitiers** and **Angoulême**—the former with its unique cathedral, the latter in its impressive site above the River **Charente**. Perhaps some of you will have explored the great port of **La Rochelle**. These are amongst the best-known tourist attractions of the region—but how many of you know the quiet, history-filled corners of the area?

Start in the **Gartempe** Valley where it joins the **Creuse** at **La Roche-Posay**—a small spa town. Eventually, I want you to arrive at **St-Savin**—but before going there I suggest you first drive down the eastern bank of the Creuse to **Le Blanc**—stopping on your way at the fine Romanesque Abbey of **Fontgombault**. Then, if you have the time, explore the **Anglin** Valley, north and south of **Mérigny** and as far as **Angles-s-l'Anglin** (with a splendid ruined castle): you will have the D50 to yourself. When you have soaked up this lovely river country head for St-Savin.

The superb Romanesque church at St-Savin is the finest example of so many in the region—the finely proportioned exterior hides the promise of the astonishing interior. The frescoes and decorations, Byzantine in origin, are thrilling sights—they should not be missed on any account by visitors to this area of France.

Continue south, on the west bank of the Gartempe, to **Montmorillon**, a picturesque old town and a perfect example of many in the region.

Now make the short hop west to **Lussac-les-Châteaux**. This small town has a sad link with the great English hero, Sir John Chandos—the general who won the battle of Poitiers in 1356. He was killed in a small skirmish, on January 1, 1379, at the bridge crossing the River **Vienne**, just west of Lussac. Research the life of this outstanding soldier—it is an interesting story.

From Lussac follow the delightful Vienne north—you will want to stop often. **Chauvigny**, with the imposing ruins of several châteaux, will make extra demands on your time but not one single second will be regretted.

Finally—I am imposing on your time even further—don't miss the châteaux at **Touffou** (north of Chauvigny, on the west bank) and **Dissay** (between Poitiers and **Châtellerault**): both are amongst the finest of the small châteaux in France.

To the west of the region are **Parthenay** and **Niort**—such old towns; important even in centuries when the English ruled Poitou. My favourites of this western corner include **Fontenay-le-Comte**, a lovely Renaissance town with woods and the River **Vendée** to the north—all of it ignored by so many. To the south is **Aulnay**, famous in the days when it was an important stopping point for the pilgrims travelling to St-Jacques-de-Compostelle. The 12th century Eglise St-Pierre is another superb example in the Poitou region of Romanesque architecture.

Between Fontenay-le-Comte and Aulnay is the quite unique **Marais Poitevin**—written about elsewhere and again not to be missed by any reader who thrives on exploring the best *hidden corners* of France.

South of La Rochelle are a variety of interesting places. **Rochefort** had great maritime importance three centuries ago; it was one of the first *planned* towns and built by Colbert. At **Fouras** a ferry will take you to the **Ile d'Aix**; Napoléon made the same journey in July 1815. It was the last time he stood on the mainland of France—a monument marks the spot. At nearby **Brouage** are the strong fortifications, built by Richelieu, for this once famous port. Now it is marshland and the sea is kilometres away. Champlain, who founded Quebec, was born here.

Marennes is famous for its oysters—it gives its name to a variety of them. Both here and at **Bourcefranc** (it has an Oyster Museum) there are acres of oyster beds.

Finally don't miss **Cognac** and its own world-famous *treasures*. Other treasures near the town are the Bénédictine abbey at **Bassac** and the castle at **Pons**.

34

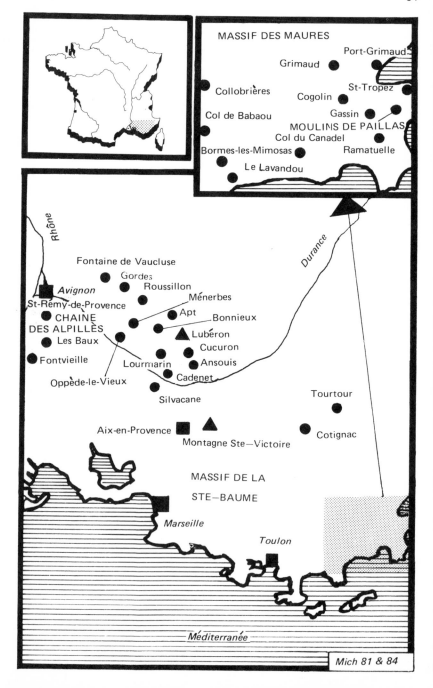

MASSIF DES MAURES

Grimaud
Port-Grimaud
Collobrières
Cogolin
St-Tropez
Col de Babaou
Gassin
MOULINS DE PAILLAS
Col du Canadel
Bormes-les-Mimosas
Ramatuelle
Le Lavandou

Rhône

Fontaine de Vaucluse
Gordes
Roussillon
Avignon
Ménerbes
St-Rémy-de-Provence
Apt
Bonnieux
CHAINE
DES ALPILLES
Lubéron
Les Baux
Cucuron
Fontvieille
Ansouis
Lourmarin
Oppède-le-Vieux
Cadenet
Silvacane
Tourtour

Aix-en-Provence
Montagne Ste—Victoire
Cotignac

MASSIF DE LA
STE—BAUME

Marseille

Toulon

Méditerranée

Mich 81 & 84

For those of you who have enjoyed the pleasures of **St-Tropez** and **Port-Grimaud**, the starting point of my tour through the quieter parts of Provence may already be known to you: the **Moulins de Paillas**—the Windmills of Paillas, in the hills south of St-Tropez. They are ruins now, but the countryside surrounding them—including the old Provençal villages of **Gassin** and **Ramatuelle**—makes it an interesting area. Fine local wines are additional bonuses.

From **Grimaud**, don't take the direct minor road to **Collobrières** (itself a highly attractive route). Instead, follow a spectacular alternative. **Cogolin** comes first, and eight kilometres later a climb up to the **Col du Canadel**—a long ribbon of coast lies below you. Now follow the narrow mountain road high above **Le Lavandou** and **Bormes-les-Mimosas** (an alluring, attractive village); in May the hills hereabouts are carpeted in wild flowers—a delightful surprise.

Next you go north through the best of the **Massif des Maures**; across the **Col de Babaou**, through Collobrières and the narrow forest roads to the north.

Two mountain areas await you; drive to the top of both if you can. The first is the **Massif de la Ste-Baume**; famous for its forest and the cave, as legend has it, where Mary Magdalene lived her last days. To the north is another famous mountain mass—Cézanne's own **Montagne Ste-Victoire**; the roads that encircle it are well worth using—before exploring that gem of a town **Aix-en-Provence**.

If you have the time, explore the quiet, attractive hills around **Cotignac** and **Tourtour**; in May they are blanketed with flowers and perfumed with the aroma of herbs.

North of Aix-en-Provence is a whole series of eye-catching treats. First aim for **Cadenet**—but on your way there make the short detour to the old ruins of a Cistercian abbey at **Silvacane**. This is in the **Durance** Valley on the southern bank. At **Lourmarin**, north of Cadenet, there is a fine château, part medieval, part Renaissance. A château with a similar past is at **Ansouis**, east of Cadenet; it has charming gardens and has been owned by the same family for centuries.

Now use the narrow lanes that lead from **Cucuron** up the steep southern slopes of the mysterious, sullen **Lubéron** Mountain. At the top, drive to the east and enjoy the splendid views from the Mourre Nègre—1125 metres high. Descend to the north, first calling at **Apt**—an old Roman town, full of interest. Then make certain your route takes you through three villages: **Bonnieux**, **Ménerbes** and **Oppède-le-Vieux**. All three have marvellous sites, interesting stories to tell of intriguing history, and all three deserve to be thoroughly explored on foot.

To the north is the amazing red and ochre village of **Roussillon**. At **Gordes** are the strange-shapes of the restored *Bories*—small buildings, looking like bee-hives, built in the Stone Age and constructed of dry-stone slabs.

To the west of Gordes is the **Fontaine de Vaucluse**—a thrilling sight in the winter and spring when the flow of water is at its strongest: it is a *resurgent spring*; having gone underground kilometres away, it shoots out its flood of water in a spectacular fashion at the point where it exits from the rock face.

The strange outcrop of rocks called the **Chaîne des Alpilles** are your next port of call. **St-Rémy-de-Provence** is a favourite small town of mine. **Les Baux** and its special attractions are written about elsewhere; Daudet's famous *Moulin* (Mill); **Fontvieille**; Les Antiques and its Roman remains; the hills and their many viewpoints—all are absorbing. Try to see the craggy hills at sunset; if you are lucky both the sky and the rocks will look like a devil's cauldron!

Finally, make certain you enjoy the special pleasure of shopping in the Provençal open-air markets; where you can buy local produce with the Provençal smell, texture and freshness—to be savoured later on a picnic in some shady spot.

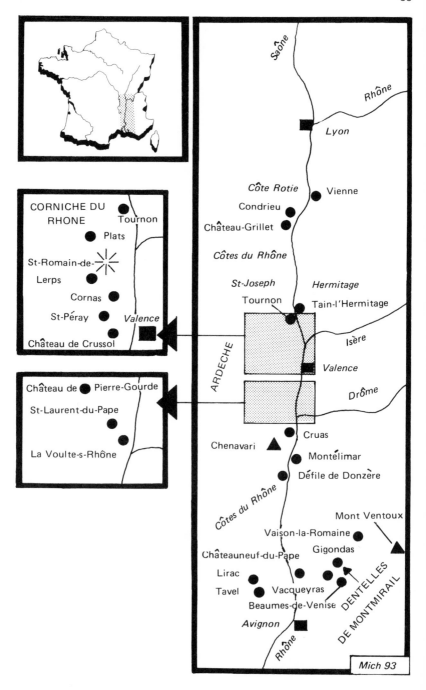

WINE COUNTRY

Wine Villages & Towns—page 39—describes some of the better-known wine-producing areas. The purpose of this chapter is to draw your attention to a stretch of country —certainly famous enough in other ways—which would reward a *new* look at it from a different perspective; its many differing wines, its vineyards and wine villages. All of it lies in or near the **Rhône** Valley—the ***Côtes du Rhône***.

I suggest you forget the A7 Autoroute and concentrate mainly on the western bank —with just the odd foray across to the other bank. Start at **Vienne** (south of Lyon); it's an old town, famous in Roman times, full of architectural treasures from that period as well as from more recent centuries. A few kilometres to the south, on the west bank, are the first vineyards of the ***Côte Rôtie*** (that means *roasted*)—magnificent red wines are made here. At **Condrieu** the colour of the vintage changes; the whites of this area and **Château-Grillet** are made from the Viognier grape (only found here)—lovely, soft white wines. These are famous throughout the world and just minute amounts are harvested: no wonder. Explore the terraced slopes (some terraces have just one or two rows of vines) and marvel at the patience and hard work of the vinegrowers working these astonishingly steep hills.

Continue south to **Tournon**, passing through the lesser-known wine area of **St-Joseph**. At Tournon, on the other bank, are the renowned vineyards on the granite hill called **Hermitage**, overlooking **Tain-l'Hermitage**.

From Tournon allow an hour or two to make a really memorable drive: full of interest, extensive views and a run that will give you a taste of a different sort—a look at the rich countryside of the **Ardèche**. Take the minor road from Tournon up into the hills— signposted **Plats** and **St-Romain-de-Lerps**; the route is called the **Corniche du Rhône**. Above St-Romain is where you will get the best of all the panoramas on this run. It finishes by descending to **St-Péray**, home of the 2000 year old white wine; Pliny wrote of it. There is a magnificent, old-gold sparkling wine—a *mousseux*—and a good still white. Like the St-Joseph wines, the **Cornas** reds (just north of St-Péray) are both undervalued and excellent. On the craggy rocks to the east of St-Péray are the ruins of the **Château de Crussol**.

Now make another short mountain-top drive—one not to be missed on any account. Near **La Voulte-s-Rhône** is **St-Laurent-du-Pape**; take the tiny D266 and climb north, higher and higher; eventually take the track to the ruins of the **Château de Pierre-Gourde**—an extensive panorama will be your reward.

Continue due south—many diversions will entice you if you have the time: **Cruas**, with its *église* and recently discovered crypts; the views from the **Chenavari** peak, west of **Montélimar**; and the **Défile de Donzère**. Notice how the scenery and vegetation changes completely; from the lush greens of the north to the dryer lands of Provence. Explore the wine villages of **Lirac** and **Tavel** (both famous for their rosé wines); cross the Rhône and let **Châteauneuf-du-Pape** be your next port of call—various grape types are combined to make its red wines the finest in the south.

Finally, aim north-east to one of my favourite, *hidden corners* of Provence: the hills to the west of **Mont Ventoux** and south of **Vaison-la-Romaine**. Start at **Beaumes-de-Venise**, the home of the honey-tasting, rich Muscat wine, made from the grape of that name. Skirting the western corner of the hills—the **Dentelles de Montmirail**—you reach **Vacqueyras**, and then, around the corner, is **Gigondas**; both make powerful red wines. There is no better corner in the south where you can absorb the feel, taste and smell of Provence: its woods and hills; its superb produce, cultivated in the cypress-lined fields; and its wide variety of excellent wines.

I hope this will spur you on to try the same idea in other regions of France—where countryside, cuisine and wines can be married to their historical heritage.

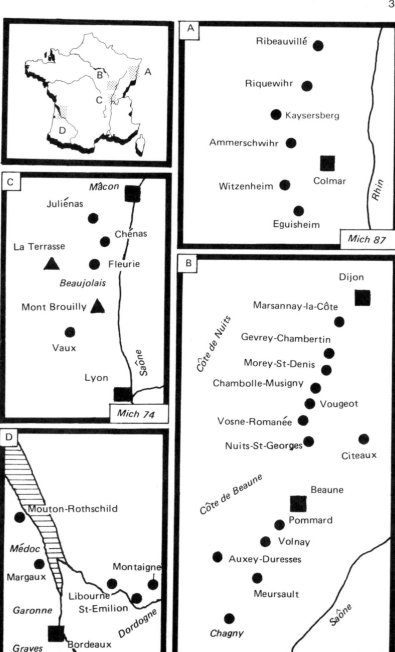

A

Ribeauvillé

Riquewihr

Kaysersberg

Ammerschwihr

Witzenheim　Colmar

Eguisheim

Rhin

Mich 87

C

Mâcon

Juliénas

Chénas

La Terrasse

Fleurie

Beaujolais

Mont Brouilly

Vaux

Lyon

Saône

Mich 74

B

Dijon

Marsannay-la-Côte

Gevrey-Chambertin

Morey-St-Denis

Chambolle-Musigny

Vougeot

Vosne-Romanée

Nuits-St-Georges

Citeaux

Côte de Nuits

Côte de Beaune

Beaune

Pommard

Volnay

Auxey-Duresses

Meursault

Chagny

Saône

Mich 66 & 70

D

Mouton-Rothschild

Médoc

Margaux

Montaigne

Libourne

St-Emilion

Garonne

Dordogne

Graves

Bordeaux

Labrède

Mich 71

Those of you who have read *French Leave* will know of my love for the cuisine and wines of France. In its pages I have managed to identify all the wines of France, and, in each one of the 20 regions, I have described the *local* wines.

Whenever you are in France, always order the *local* or *regional* wines—there is no more effective way of discovering the pleasures of those *local* wines than by exploring the villages and their neighbouring vineyards in wine-producing areas. To give you an encouraging start, I am going to suggest you begin with four of the better-known areas, where, apart from the wine villages in each of them, there are many other interesting scenic and historical sights to see and enjoy.

Alsace is without doubt the area with the most picturesque wine villages: **Ribeauvillé**, **Riquewihr**, **Kaysersberg**, **Ammerschwihr**, **Witzenheim** and **Eguisheim** are a few you will find on the *Route du Vin*. Riquewihr, a medieval town, is the jewel amongst them, rich in old buildings and streets. Albert Schweitzer was born at Kaysersberg—an old town which has always been important, back to Roman times. Ammerschwihr was badly damaged during the war—but was quickly and sensitively rebuilt. Eguisheim is a delight—walk the lanes with their flower-laden balconies.

Colmar is hardly a village—but it is fitting that it should be included. It's one of my favourite towns—full of treasures: timber houses from the 16th century; the Musée d'Unterlinden; the Maison Pfister; an area called *Little Venice*; and, for the benefit of tourists, pedestrian-only streets in the town centre.

The many differing gems of Burgundy have rightly won many references in this small book: the wine villages and towns deserve a chapter of their own!

The *Côte de Nuits* is where you must start; at **Marsannay-la-Côte**. This village is known for its rosé wine, though the villages that quickly follow—with household names—are the homes of the world's greatest red wines: **Gevrey-Chambertin**, **Morey-St-Denis**; **Chambolle-Musigny**; **Vougeot** (visit the historic château, the Clos de Vougeot, founded by monks from **Citeaux** Abbey—page 53); **Vosne-Romanée** (is there any more expensive ground anywhere in the world?) and **Nuits-St-Georges**.

Further south is the *Côte de Beaune*; the great white Burgundies come from this area. **Pommard**, **Volnay**, **Auxey-Duresses** and **Meursault** are some of the villages.

The two world-famous Burgundian towns of **Dijon** and **Beaune** deserve some of your daytime hours. The old area of Dijon surrounding the Place de la Liberation and the many museums (particularly the Beaux Arts) should not be missed.

The same is true of the treasures of **Beaune**: the Hospices de Beaune, the Hôtel-Dieu and the Musée du Vin de Bourgogne are the highlights, but any ramble through the inner-town, and the ramparts surrounding it, is well worthwhile.

North of **Lyon** and west of the River **Saône** are the wooded hills of **Beaujolais** country; quiet roads take you through sleepy villages which are a roll call of Beaujolais wines—**Fleurie**, **Chénas** and **Juliénas** are examples. Don't miss **Vaux**, the original *Clochemerle*; or the views from the top of **Mont Brouilly** and from **La Terrasse**, near Fleurie; or the peaceful hills to the west.

The fourth and final area is **Bordeaux**. Scenically it is all pretty dull; don't let that deter you seeing the famous châteaux of the **Médoc** (especially **Margaux** and **Mouton-Rothschild**) and **Graves** (particularly the attractive **Labrède** and its lovely park). Spend time in Bordeaux, bustling with a host of attractions. Follow the roads on the eastern bank of the **Garonne**—then go north to **St-Emilion** with its glorious site, its ramparts and its extraordinary monolithic church, hewn out of the rocky cliffs by the disciples of the 8th century St-Emilion. Nearby **Libourne**, the biggest of the *bastides* (fortified towns), is where the Black Prince was born; Michel de Montaigne, the philosopher, was born at the Château de **Montaigne**.

40

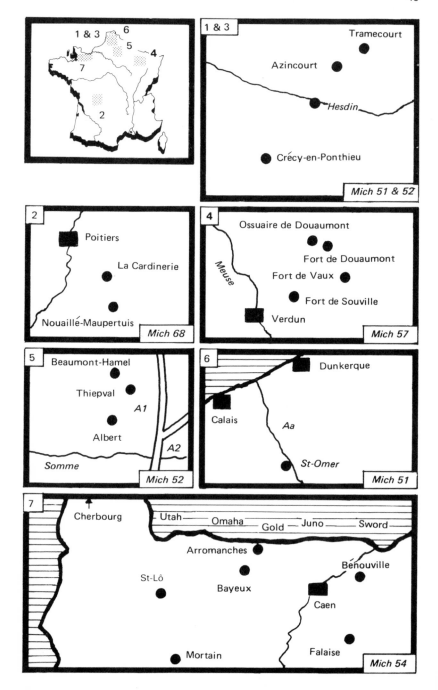

My selections cover many centuries in time: all of them require you to use your imagination—all history expects that of you! With the help of large-scale maps, studied intelligently, and perhaps more detailed accounts of the battles themselves, a picture of each of them will form most clearly in your mind—some lasted just hours, some months and some years.

Crécy (1). From a small mound, just north of **Crécy-en-Ponthieu** (1 kilometre on D111), you, too, can survey the same scene Edward III saw on August 26, 1346. It was at the start of the Hundred Years War and for the first time, and not the last, the French learned the bitter lesson of the stunning use made by the English—and the Welsh—of the longbow. It also marked the day that cannonballs were first used in battle: a pile of them lie in a small museum at the village.

Poitiers (2). On September 19, 1356, one of the outstanding English victories of the Middle Ages was at **Poitiers**. The battle was fought at **La Cardinerie**, just before reaching **Nouaillé-Maupertuis**. Edward, the Black Prince, took the credit for the victory but it was Sir John Chandos who masterminded it all.

Agincourt (3). 69 years after Crécy another spectacular and bloody battle was lost by the French at Agincourt (**Azincourt** on the maps)—just 30 kilometres to the north-east! The spot is marked on the D104 and even today you can see why, once again, the French nobles were massacred by the longbowmen: they had no room for manoeuvre, caught as they were between the woods of Azincourt and **Tramecourt**.

Verdun (4). A unique, symbolic name that means so much to France: a symbol of French valour—a symbol of French suffering. To the north-east of **Verdun** are the tragic reminders of the bitter battles that raged there during the First World War: the **Fort de Douaumont**, the **Fort de Vaux**, the **Fort de Souville**, monuments, cemeteries and the chilling **Ossuaire** (Ossuary) **de Douaumont**. It is all sombre, sacred ground: the scars of Verdun influenced French thinking profoundly during the ensuing 25 years.

The Somme (5). Elizabeth Nicholas wrote—'who could make truly merry in a town that bore the name Peronne?' The land north of the River **Somme** and surrounding **Albert** was the scene of the worst bloodshed of the 1914–18 war. Motorists speeding along the A1, at the point the A2 joins it, pass this consecrated ground in less than five minutes and yet . . . what countless sacrifices were made in those cold, bleak fields. Stop one day at the memorials at **Thiepval** and **Beaumont-Hamel** and contemplate the awful sufferings of previous generations. The best guide is *Before Endeavours Fade* by Rose Coombs (published by After the Battle).

Dunkirk (6). If you use **Calais** or **Dunkerque** as ports of embarkation, don't sit out the last hours in the terminal car parks. Spend the time in the lanes of the canal and dyke-lined terrain to the south of Dunkerque. You will get a first-hand picture of what an important part that marshy piece of Flanders played in the successful evacuation from Dunkerque; in the way it helped the retreating forces to defend their positions during those few vital days; and how the fear of the marshes influenced the Germans in their decision, made on May 23, 1940, to temporarily stop their tanks at the River **Aa**, to the west of the port.

D-Day Landings (7). On the Normandy coast, north of **Bayeux** and **Caen** are the D-Day beaches of **Utah**, **Omaha**, **Gold**, **Juno** and **Sword** (west to east). See the museum at **Arromanches**. At **Bénouville** is Pegasus Bridge, where, on the night of June 5/6, 1944, ahead of the landing, airborne troops parachuted down. Normandy suffered terribly during those first few weeks. Arm yourself with one of the many books that tell the story of those days: then follow, step by step, the battles that raged for **St-Lô**, **Caen**, **Cherbourg**, **Mortain** and **Falaise**. Dozens of cemeteries, throughout Normandy, remind you of the high price the Allies paid to win those battles.

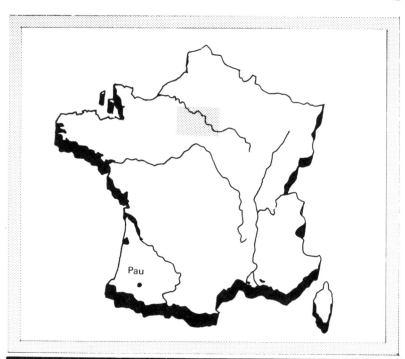

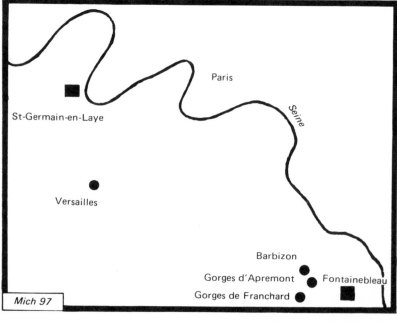

St-Germain-en-Laye

Versailles

Paris

Seine

Barbizon

Gorges d'Apremont

Gorges de Franchard

Fontainebleau

Mich 97

Pau

A hero of France and the very symbol of French unity: Henry was one of France's greatest kings and one of her greatest men. His life and story is worth studying (1553–1610): he was a passionate builder and there are many sites and buildings associated with him throughout France. Visit some of them and through the marvel of your imagination visualise the times and importance of this fine man.

> *"But out spake gentle Henry, 'No Frenchman is my foe:*
> *Down, down with every foreigner, but let your brethren go.' "*

So wrote Macaulay on the battle of Ivry. Henry was brought up as a Protestant, and in the fiery partisan Béarn country. His *conversions* have become famous—but he thought of Frenchmen as Frenchmen, whatever their creed. He was the catalyst that unified France in the 16th century—much of his work was undone in later years. Three towns—all associated with him—are worth your time.

Pau was his birthplace. The château in this lovely town, with its exquisite grace and Edwardian elegance, is full of reminders of his birth and early days. But the town is endowed with many other charms; amongst them the classic Boulevard des Pyrénées —with its view of the majestic mountains to the south—and its pretty parks. We have seen the area in early April: the fresh green buds and blossom everywhere and the snow-capped peaks sparkling in the sharp clear air. The countryside, in every direction, deserves your time; it is not a corner of France where you are likely to be swamped by thousands of tourists.

The Château of **St-Germain-en-Laye**—in its present form—was the creation of Henry IV. Sitting above the **Seine**, with views of **Paris** to the east and fine forests stretching away to the north, it was the perfect site for a château. It was incomplete when he became King. All manner of remarkable things can be seen at the château, in the surrounding gardens—designed by Lenôtre—and in the town of St-Germain. A special treasure is the forest; consider yourself particularly fortunate if you can see it in the mellow month of October, when it is at its very best. Debussy was born in the town in 1862; a statue commemorates the event.

Henry IV contributed a great deal to the development of **Fontainebleau**, the most human of the Royal residences. Its Renaissance style is so much more acceptable than **Versailles**; the latter is impressive, awesome and massive—but it lacks the atmosphere of Fontainebleau. Henry IV was not the only French king to leave his mark on this precious corner of France. Francis I (particularly so), Henry II, Catherine de Medici, Louis XIV and Napoléon were all involved with it during its long history. Napoléon welcomed Pope Pious VII here in 1804 when he came to crown him; he then imprisoned him at Fontainebleau in 1812. It was here also he made his famous farewell to his guard, after his first abdication in 1814.

One of the most intriguing aspects of any visit is to visualise the goings-on during those centuries in this, the most secretive and most atmospheric of châteaux. This is where history really comes alive. Like St-Germain, an added bonus is the marvellous forest, sitting like a giant green sea to the west of the town, where it is the easiest thing in the world to lose yourself completely in those leafy glades.

Hidden in the forest are two gems—created by Nature—that you must make the effort to see. Both are easily reached by car—but a certain amount of walking is necessary if you are to fully enjoy them: the **Gorges d'Apremont**, near **Barbizon**, and the **Gorges de Franchard**, a little further south. Both are areas where hundreds of huge rocks combine together with the surrounding woods of pine, oak and beech to form an unusual and amazing picture. Do search them out.

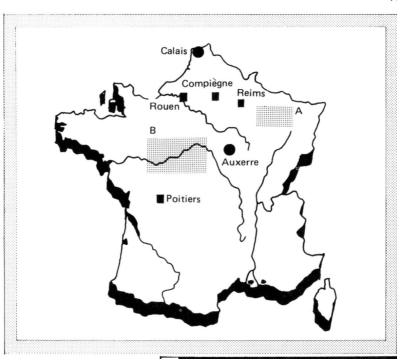

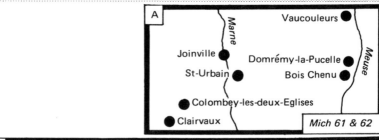

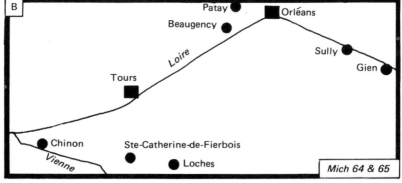

JOURNEYS OF JOAN OF ARC

Hammond Innes, writing about **Chinon**, made the telling comment that it was in the fortress there that the death knell of English power in France was sounded, when Joan of Arc met the Dauphin for the first time.

There is no more absorbing way of bringing history alive than by reading Joan's story and following her footsteps during that short, majestic and inspiring life. It is well worth finding the time to trace once again those momentous months.

Start at **Domrémy-la-Pucelle** where she was born. The house is there, much restored, but the living room and its fireplace, her bedroom, the garden—none of these can have changed much. On a hill nearby, at **Bois Chenu**, south of the village—where she first heard the voices—is a Basilica, built in her honour.

It was Robert de Baudricourt at **Vaucouleurs**, 20 kilometres north of Domrémy, who sent her to see the Dauphin. The Porte de France, through which Joan rode on February 23, 1429 to start her momentous journey, is still there.

She travelled for 11 days: going through **Joinville** (she slept at nearby **St-Urbain** on the first night) and then on to **Clairvaux**, now a prison, but once such an important abbey. (You should not miss visiting the home of another legend of France—Général-de-Gaulle—at nearby **Colombey-les-deux-Eglises**.) Then she went on past **Auxerre** (later returning through this lovely old town with Charles on their way to his coronation at Reims), **Gien** and **Loches**.

Few people take the trouble to locate **Ste-Catherine-de-Fierbois**, just off the N10, 25 kilometres south of **Tours**. You can still see the place where Joan spent the night and the old church where Charles Martel's sword was found—a mysterious story, unexplained to this day. Could it have been his sword? Hardly, as some 700 years had elapsed since his death. How did she know it was there?

Today the fortress at Chinon is in ruins but much of the town Joan saw still stands. She rode under the Tour de l'Horloge, stayed first at the Grand Carroi and later in the Château du Coudray, the western part of the castle. She was sent to **Poitiers** to be examined by doctors. At last the Dauphin, not surprisingly, as **Orléans** was in mortal danger, sent her up the **Loire** with her own army.

There is not much in Orléans today that remains of Joan's time. But, at **Sully** there is; Joan was a guest at the château there on two occasions. It was during her first visit after the battles of Orléans, **Beaugency** and **Patay** (where Talbot was captured), that she persuaded the Dauphin to go to **Reims** to be crowned.

It is not difficult to relive that coronation in the magnificent Gothic cathedral. Your imagination will help you to envisage that stirring moment when she threw herself at the feet of Charles VII. It was at **Compiègne** that the English captured Joan; she was shut outside the town gates by her own soldiers, in their haste to retreat. Remains of the ramparts, near the Palais, are still there.

Rouen is where Saint Joan, only 19, was burnt at the stake on May 30, 1431. In 1931 some of the most distinguished people in the U.K., Catholics and non-Catholics alike, supported an appeal to provide a window in her memory in Rouen Cathedral. In 1956, 500 years after her trial was declared null and void and she was proclaimed innocent, that window, by Max Ingrand, was dedicated on the reopening of Rouen Cathedral after the war.

The English who watched her die said; "We are lost; we have burnt a Saint." It was in the years that followed that the French began to think of themselves as Frenchmen, not Burgundians, Normans and Armagnacs. By 1453, the English had been routed from France: only **Calais** remained in their hands.

Only a few days—in this modern age—would be needed to follow Joan's steps. Ideally, allow a week; there are many other sights to see on the journey.

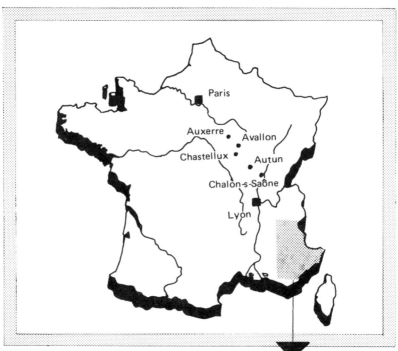

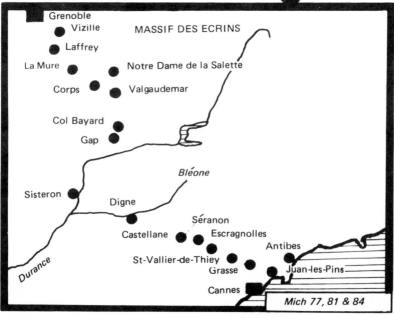

Mich 77, 81 & 84

On March 1, 1815, Napoléon landed at **Juan-les-Pins** with his small army of about 1000 men. He had set out from Elba just four days before to recapture the Empire he had lost a year earlier. He could never have believed how easily he would achieve that objective: the weeks that followed tell an interesting story.

Juan was a fortunate place to land, hidden as it was from the forts at **Antibes** and **Cannes** by the Cap d'Antibes and the Pointe de la Croisette. The South was Royalist so Napoléon hurried north. There are many examples in history of how quickly human reactions can change: Napoléon's story is a classic example. He was called the *Corsican Adventurer* on landing, the *Usurper* by the time he reached **Digne**, *Bonaparte* at **Grenoble**, *Napoléon* at **Chalon-s-Saône** and *Emperor* at **Auxerre**. By March 21, on reaching **Paris**, he was honoured as *His Royal and Imperial Majesty*!

The first days of that return were eventful ones indeed. The road he followed from **Grasse** to Grenoble has long been called by his name—the *Route de Napoléon.* He bypassed Grasse, a Royalist town, was welcomed at **Escragnolles** and spent his first night at the Château de Brondet at **Séranon**. He had covered more than 50 kilometres on that first day. At **St-Vallier-de-Thiey**, north-west of Grasse, a monument commemorates that eventful 24 hours. He continued on through tough, mountainous country: first **Castellane**, then Digne, where the going became easier.

He followed the River **Bléone** on its northern bank and then turned north into the mighty **Durance** Valley. Soon he reached **Sisteron**, a fortified town, built in the days of Henry IV and lying under a high rock face that appears to curtain-off the entire valley. It was at Sisteron that he got his first real welcome.

Beyond Sisteron the vegetation and other aspects of the countryside changed quickly and dramatically; from the dry lands of Provence to greener, more Alpine-like scenes. He went on through **Gap**—a dull, dour place—and up the **Col Bayard**; most of the population went with him for the first few kilometres.

Then Napoléon marched north through **Corps** and **La Mure**. You should take the chance to explore the narrow roads to the west of the N85 and the valleys striking up into the high mountains of the **Massif des Ecrins** to the east. The valley called **Valgaudemar** is certainly worthy of your time, as is the memorable shrine of **Notre Dame de la Salette**, high in the mountains, north of Corps (page 75).

Between La Mure and **Laffrey** are three lakes; on the banks of the northernmost one is a monument commemorating perhaps one of the most important events of his life. Delassart, a Royalist officer, had chosen to defend the pass to the north; easily done by determined troops. But Napoléon defied them bravely; marched within firing distance, and not one of the Royalists fired when the order was given.

"I am your Emperor—kill me," he said. The defending troops deserted their positions, saluted their Emperor and joined forces with him.

Napoléon descended into **Vizille**, the town where the Revolution is said to have begun in 1788; he was welcomed royally.

By **Grenoble** an entire Royalist regiment led by Charles de Labedozère (an interesting individual from **Chastellux** in the Morvan—his story is worth researching) had joined him and again the defending troops ignored the order to fire on the advancing Bonapartist men. He captured the town with no loss of life.

Lyon put up no resistance at all. He stayed one night at the Hôtel St-Louis in **Autun** (he had been educated at the College there) and another night at the Chapeau Rouge in **Avallon**. A final attempt to stop him could have been made by Marshal Ney at **Auxerre** but, confused at first, he too eventually joined forces with Napoléon. A successful seal was put on Napoléon's return when he reviewed Ney's troops in the Place St-Etienne, on the west side of Auxerre Cathedral.

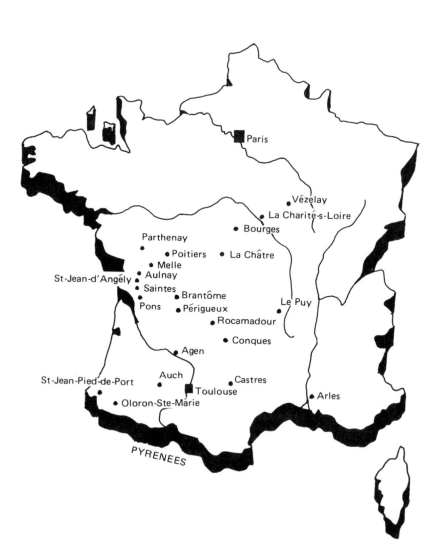

Paris

Vézelay

La Charité-s-Loire

Bourges

Parthenay

Poitiers

La Châtre

Melle

Aulnay

St-Jean-d'Angély

Saintes

Brantôme

Le Puy

Pons

Périgueux

Rocamadour

Conques

Agen

Auch

Castres

St-Jean-Pied-de-Port

Toulouse

Oloron-Ste-Marie

Arles

PYRENEES

There were many alternative routes across France that pilgrims used on their long journeys to Santiago de Compostela in northern Spain. The four main starting points were at **Vézelay**, **Le Puy**, **Paris** and **Arles**; each of the routes followed a general line though all of them had small variations within them. I will identify some of the most important religious ports of call on those routes; try to visit as many of them as you can—all are situated in lovely countryside.

The **Vézelay** route included many of the important churches and abbeys described elsewhere in this book: **La Charité-s-Loire**, **Bourges**, **La Châtre**, **Brantôme** and **Périgueux** amongst them. Seek them out when you are travelling in their vicinity.

The road from **Arles** included stops at **Castres**, **Toulouse** and **Auch**. Do spare time for the cathedral at Auch—it has magnificent choir stalls, thought to be amongst the finest in France. This southerly route crossed the **Pyrénées** just south of **Oloron-Ste-Marie**. Two churches here were important to the pilgrims: the 13th century Eglise Ste-Marie, which has a fine doorway; and the Church of Ste-Croix.

I will describe the other two routes in more detail—for, even today, there are a dozen or more marvellous sites on them which certainly merit your attention. Start at **Le Puy**—one of the most unusual towns in France. Sharp needles of volcanic rock rise on all sides, several of them having chapels and statues on their summits. The most needle-like has the Chapelle St-Michel d'Aiguilhe on its peak—a Romanesque chapel worthy of the 267 steps climb to reach it. Another outcrop has the huge statue of Notre Dame de France on its summit. But it was the cathedral and its famous black Virgin of Le Puy that drew the pilgrims there. Equally important was the *pierre aux fièvres*; a piece of black stone with miraculous healing powers. The cathedral is a strange mixture of Byzantine and Romanesque; the cloisters are particularly cool, quiet and inspiring and are amongst the finest in France.

Conques was a stopping point on the Le Puy route. It is lost in the hills south of the River Lot; even today it will reward your efforts to find it. The Romanesque church is remarkable—its *treasure*, even more so. Sainte Foy was a young Christian martyr; her relics were at **Agen**, where they worked miracles. Legend has it that a monk from Conques worked faithfully at Agen for 10 years, then removed the relics to Conques, where they have since remained. One of the items making up the *treasure* is a statue of Ste-Foy, carved in yew and covered with gold and precious stones—a brilliant example of the work of goldsmiths, centuries ago.

Some pilgrims made a detour to **Rocamadour**. It has a spectacular site, hugging the north side of a steep valley. It is the statue of the Virgin Mary, carved from oak and now ebony coloured through the passage of time, that drew the pilgrims here; included amongst them were two Kings of England—Henry II and John. More recently, the composer Poulenc rediscovered his Christian faith at Rocamadour.

Let's pick up the **Paris** route at **Parthenay**, in Poitou. Here the name St-Jacques is given to a bridge, a gate and a splendid old street. **Poitiers** and **Melle** were important stops on the road south. Beyond Melle is the marvellous Romanesque church at **Aulnay**; it has a great number of exquisite sculptures. Not too far away is **St-Jean-d'Angély**; its Bénédictine abbey was destroyed during the Religious Wars but it was restored in part and it has stayed like that to this day.

Then the pilgrims went on through **Saintes**, once the capital of Western Gaul; it is full of treasures, particularly its Romanesque churches. The old town; the river; the atmospheric spirit of the place; all still combine in an inspiring way. **Pons** came next with its great castle keep and hospice.

The Paris, Vézelay and Le Puy routes met at **St-Jean-Pied-de-Port**; in the vicinity of this Pyrénées town are many pilgrimage sites, all clearly marked.

50

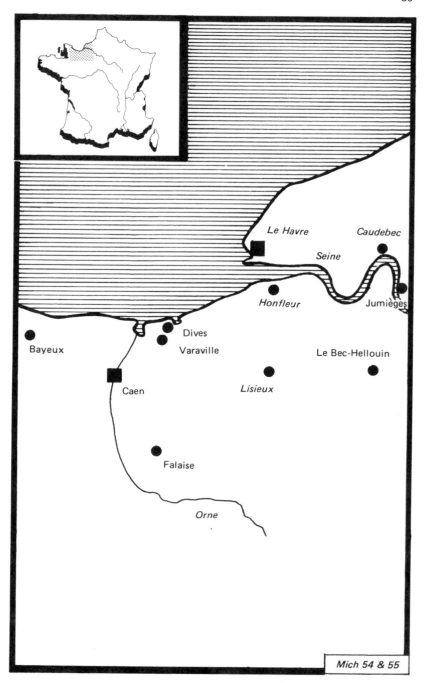

Mich 54 & 55

WILLIAM THE CONQUEROR

The Norman Conquest brought about a series of important consequences for both England and Western Europe. It marked the beginning of the growth of unity in Great Britain—though that is hardly complete, even today. It saw, in time, the forming of a fine, compound language. It is worth spending a little time in those places in Normandy, associated with William, to capture the spirit of those days.

In 911 Vikings settled in this part of France. From those simple beginnings the Norman dukedom grew. William was born in 1027 and by the time he was a teenager he had already survived several assassination attempts. He matured into a man with outstanding qualities: he had courage, spirit and strength; he was a great fighter and leader of men: he was severe and hard; and above all he was a political master. He was used to getting what he wanted.

The **Bayeux** tapestry—in reality a 70 metres length of embroidered linen—tells the story of the Conquest. It starts with the visit of Harold to Normandy in 1064. At that time Edward the Confessor was still King of England; the fateful moment for Harold came when, in Bayeux Cathedral, he made an oath to William to help him win the English throne. Harold broke that promise when Edward died on January 5, 1066—being crowned himself the next day! His defeat at the hands of William came on October 14 of the same year. On Christmas Day, 10 weeks later, William himself was crowned King of England at Westminster Abbey.

William was born at the castle in **Falaise**. One entertaining way of hearing the story of William is by attending a *son et lumière* (sound and light) performance there; you will hear how Robert, William's father, just 17, fell in love with Arlette, the farmer's daughter, who was even younger. It is said he first saw her from a window in the castle, washing clothes in a pool below the walls—probably so, as the medieval wash houses are still there. What is a fact, however, is that William was born a bastard. The castle suffered terribly during the Second World War as the Germans retreated in August 1944; it has long since been restored. Falaise is a delightful place from which to explore the nearby country.

The story of how William courted Matilda, his wife, is an amusing one. She, too, reminded him of his unhappy arrival in the world; "I would rather take the veil than be wed to a bastard," she said. Eventually she relented and they were married. The Pope excommunicated them; it was Lanfranc, in 1059, who got the excommunication lifted. William and Matilda had got away with it—the price they paid was the building of two superb masterpieces in **Caen**—the Abbaye aux Dames and the Abbaye aux Hommes. Caen was William's citadel—in 1060 he fortified it with over 1000 metres of huge walls and ramparts. The whole city is well worth exploring.

Dives is where William assembled his fleet. The old port is silted up now but it must have been an amazing sight to see the 700 vessels which were built for the invasion. 15000 men sailed in that fleet—3000 of them were mounted knights. (900 years later an invasion came from the opposite direction.) The area south of Dives was important in other ways: the vast amount of timber needed for that fleet came from the forests to the south. A decade before Hastings, William had massacred the armies of Henry I of France at nearby **Varaville**.

The Abbey of **Le Bec-Hellouin** had important links with the story of William. Lanfranc, an Italian, who was William's most trusted advisor, taught at Bec. He was appointed Archbishop of Canterbury and was virtual ruler of England in those early days when William was back in Normandy. He was followed at Canterbury by Anselm, another Italian, and the then Abbot of Bec.

Don't bypass the magnificent **Jumièges** Abbey—a ruin today, it was the prototype of the great English abbeys built by William and his ancestors.

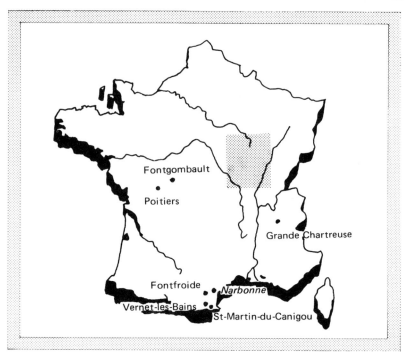

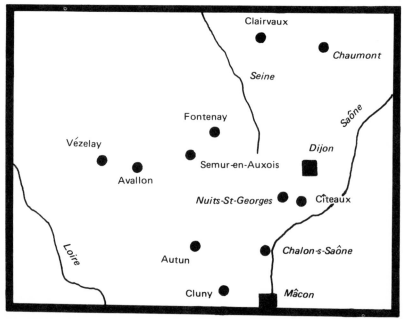

ANCIENT ABBEYS

There are dozens throughout France deserving of your time: my selection is made from just a few that span the centuries. They range from ruins to huge impressive buildings: some are easy to find, others are well off the beaten track.

Cluny—from the 9th to the 12th century—was the spiritual hub of the Christian World. Today, little remains of the Abbey of Cluny which, until the building of St-Peter's in Rome, was the largest Christian church in Europe. Its influence—spiritual, intellectual and artistic—was far-reaching; it radiated from Burgundy, throughout France and into the rest of Europe. Its hundreds of *children* (dependent abbeys and priories) kept alive the Christian faith during periods of history when it came close to dying. Perhaps only your imagination can bring alive the past majesty of the site; but both the small town and the Musée Ochier are interesting enough to warrant a detour. Some examples of the sculpture and statuary are in the museum—better examples of the Cluniac school are found at **Vézelay**, **Autun**, **Semur-en-Auxois** and **Avallon**. Don't miss the fine specimens in all these towns.

Cîteaux was the first of the Cistercian abbeys: like Cluny, only ruins remain, lying amongst the reeds, of this once powerful abbey. It, too, had hundreds of *children*, spread throughout Europe. Cîteaux was founded at the end of the 11th century, but it took Saint Bernard to build up its strong and real influence throughout Europe. A present-day order of the Cistercians are at Cîteaux now: every Sunday morning you can hear their Gregorian chants in the abbey chapel.

In 1146 it was Saint Bernard who preached so effectively for the Second Crusade to take place. **Clairvaux** was *his* abbey: today it is the site of a prison; but in the neighbourhood are reminders of the many legends that still remain, centuries later. He was the arch-enemy of Abelard who courted Heloïse so passionately. Their story is mentioned elsewhere but, coincidentally, Abelard died at Cluny.

Saint Bernard's influence was astonishing: he was the arbiter between Popes; he was the arbiter of Europe. He led the development of the Cistercian order from the abbey at Cîteaux, where he died in 1153.

Fontenay was founded in 1118 by two of Saint Bernard's uncles and it is a perfect example of the flowering of the Cistercian influence. It was the second *daughter* of Clairvaux and there is no finer place for you to grasp just why Burgundy, the mother of all the arts, became so important. That Burgundian influence lasted hundreds of years; today, Fontenay survives it all and remains in marvellous condition; it should be high on your list of essential visits to make in Burgundy.

I will let no opportunity pass which allows me the chance to persuade you to visit the majestic Massif de la Chartreuse; some of the finest mountain country in France. The **Grande Chartreuse**—in reality a monastery, not an abbey—is set in glorious scenery. Founded in 1035 by Saint Bruno of the Carthusian Order, it was destroyed and rebuilt many times during the centuries. Drive and walk the narrow forest tracks to the south of the D520B; you will have the most enjoyable views—and you will feel for yourself the special nature of this remote, secret place

St-Martin-du-Canigou is a tiny abbey, built in the 10th century, and sits high above **Vernet-les-Bains** in the eastern end of the Pyrénées. It will be an exhausting climb to reach it but the rewards will more than outweigh the effort required.

Fontfroide, to the north, near **Narbonne**, is another Cistercian abbey; it has an isolated site and sits in a small valley. The combination of silence, gardens, cloisters and old abbey makes it an inspiring place.

East of **Poitiers** is the ancient Abbey of **Fontgombault**, alongside the River Creuse. It was built at the end of the 11th century. The abbey church is a fine example of Romanesque skill; visitors can hear Gregorian chants every morning.

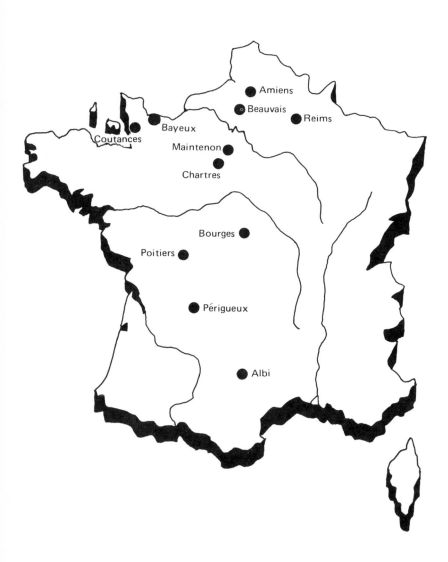

CATHEDRALS

France has given the world some priceless gifts over the centuries: amongst them are 40 or so superb cathedrals, built hundreds of years ago. Many of them took a century or more to construct—at a time when no mechanical help existed. To the present-day visitor they represent, more vividly than any literature can ever do, the spirit, faith and vitality of the people of France during those turbulent, *awakening* years. History, maps and imagination go hand in hand: all the cathedrals of France—although I record just a handful of the famous ones—are worthy of your contemplation. Use your imagination to return to those exciting times.

Amongst the famous cathedrals, be sure to visit these four: it has been said that the nave of **Amiens**, the choir of **Beauvais**, the spires at **Chartres**, and the façade of **Reims**, if all combined together, would form the *perfect* cathedral!

Amiens, like Coventry, was terribly damaged during the last war—but, miraculously, the Gothic cathedral was untouched. It is one of the largest in the world and within it are some priceless treasures. The nave is massive; because of its great height, sunlight pours in—it is not a dark, mysterious place. The stonework and sculptures are especially intriguing: a mixture of Saints, Bible figures, country animals and so on. The 110 choir stalls, the glorious windows and the celebrated Beau Dieu (a statue of Christ), all stir the heart and soul of any visitor.

Beauvais is almost as huge as Amiens; the fantastic Gothic choir is an overpowering sight. The double flying buttresses, the tapestries and the windows (including work by Max Ingrand) are amongst the treasures at Beauvais.

What words can I use to persuade you not to bypass **Chartres**—a wonder of mankind. Drive out of your way to approach it from the north-east—from the direction of **Maintenon**. Apart from the great sight of the spires, it is the statuary work and the stained-glass windows which make this cathedral such an inspiration.

The western façade, a Gothic masterpiece, is the special treasure at **Reims**. It was at Reims that all the Kings of France were crowned—it took 300 years to complete and is the most sacred building in France.

Less well-known cathedrals are spread across the length of the country.

Though **Bayeux** is more famous—its cathedral visited by those travellers wanting to see the Tapestry—**Coutances** is the best example of Gothic simplicity. It has marvellous towers and a superb lantern; Vauban insisted a carpet be laid for him so he could lie on it and contemplate the lantern at his leisure.

Poitiers is another remarkable building; this one is a Romanesque structure with considerable Byzantine influences in its stonework and construction. Though Charles Martel had defeated the Saracen armies near Poitiers, it was Levantine merchants who brought their influence to bear, centuries later, at Poitiers.

The cathedral at **Albi** is well off the normal tourist paths. The red brick building is more like a fortress and it dominates the town. It has a glorious interior—full of frescoes and statuary and a fine choir, surrounded by a beautiful stone screen. Don't pass it by.

Bourges is another vast, magnificent structure—dominating the town. It, too, lies away from the main tourist arteries—what a pity, as its colossal size, its façade, its superb stained-glass windows and its statuary rival its famous northern neighbour at Chartres. When the sun streams through those windows, enchanting, complex patterns are weaved along the nave and choir. Don't drive past this perfect example of the French heritage; unhappily, most people miss it.

The inhabitants of **Périgueux** claim that 17000 people can stand in their huge cathedral! Sir Christopher Wren was inspired by much of what he saw in France (not Italy) and it is said that the great size of St-Front may have motivated him to construct the vast dome of St Paul's Cathedral in London.

56

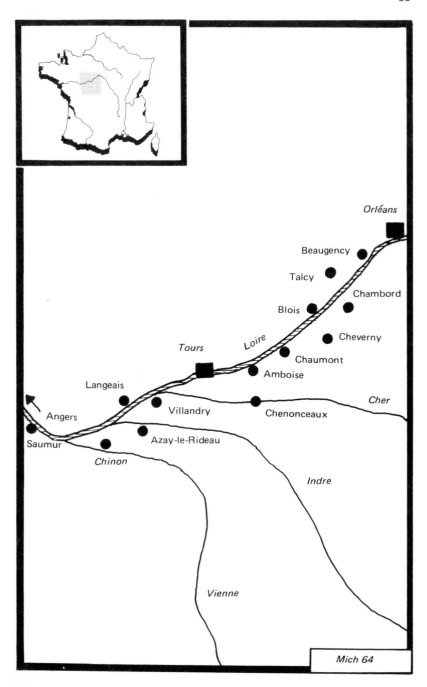

Mich 64

CHATEAUX COUNTRY

Where do I begin in this magical part of France? Foolishly I ignored it for so long—don't make the same mistake. Elsewhere in this book I write about some of the hidden treasures of the area that most visitors ignore. Balzac wrote some of the finest descriptions of this bejewelled corner of France; it is full of gems. Any other words written since are an anti-climax, after his descriptive skill.

There are 100 or more châteaux in the area. Those listed here are amongst the ones you should not miss. It is a subjective list, a personal choice—of course; but my aim is to encourage you and to give you the keys to the pleasures of the Loire and all France. See them all in daylight—but, whatever you do, do not on any account miss some of the *son et lumière* (sound and light) evening spectaculars.

Azay-le-Rideau is my favourite—a gorgeous little place. It has the perfect setting —alongside the **Indre** with water, parks and woods surrounding it. It has little history but its setting more than makes up for that.

The château at **Villandry** is pure Renaissance; the building is interesting but it is the gardens that you must explore—formalised displays covering acres of ground. It is the harmony of these gardens, together with the château, that makes Villandry a special pleasure. Many of the other châteaux, with gardens falling into neglect, have lost the overall charm that Villandry has in great measure.

Cheverny is privately-owned and a model of classical lightness, elegance and attractive lines; it was built in the 17th century and is surrounded by a park and woods. The interior is especially interesting—both decorations and furniture are amongst the finest in the Loire. In the park surrounding the château, there are kennels where the hounds of the local hunt are kept—children and adults alike will get pleasure from this *different* attraction.

The château at **Amboise** sits high above the town with glorious views of the **Loire** from the terraces. It was once part of a much greater number of buildings and originally it was built as a fortress, separated from the town. The history of Amboise is part of the history of France—full of bloodshed and tragic events. Charles VIII and François I take the credit for the construction of the château—there is much Italian influence in what you will see there.

Every one of the Loire châteaux is different from the rest; the difference at **Chenonceaux** is the sight of the classical lines of the gracious building, sitting as it does astride the River **Cher**. It has a marvellous interior with tapestries, furniture and panelling; it is sometimes known as *The Château of Six Women* and is the most visited château in France, after Fontainebleau. But you must brave the crowds and go—try it at lunchtime when it remains open and is much quieter.

Chambord is the largest of all the châteaux and is surrounded by a vast forest. From a distance the towers, the turrets, the gables and the hundreds of Renaissance chimneys make it appear like a far-off city.

Langeais is a dark, massive fortress—built in the Middle Ages and quite unlike any of the other châteaux described here. Children will love it as it has all the trappings of an impregnable fort: huge drawbridge, portcullis, formidable round towers and battlements. It sits right in the middle of the town.

Chaumont is another favourite of mine, high above the Loire in a forest-like park. Its setting, like Azay, is an extra bonus. But don't miss the furnished rooms, the stables and the intriguing stories the château can tell of Catherine de Medici and Dianne de Poitiers—two of the ladies who influenced its development.

Other châteaux should be enjoyed: **Blois**, **Angers** and **Saumur** are amongst the larger, better-known ones; the château at **Beaugency** (don't miss the town) and the château at **Talcy** (north-east of Blois) are two of the best small ones.

58

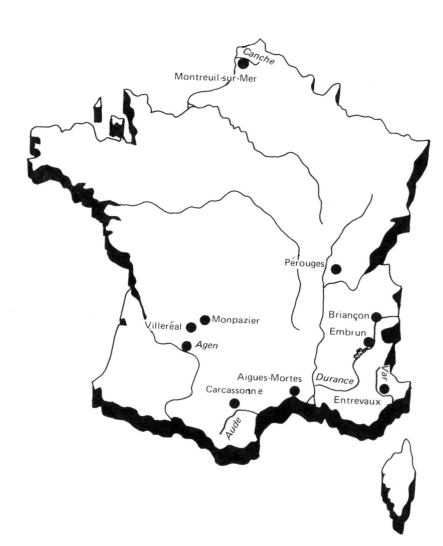

FORTIFIED TOWNS

There are dozens of these throughout France: some are huge places, some are tiny; some restored, some in ruins; but not one of them in my list will disappoint you.

Carcassonne—is there a more romantic skyline anywhere in France? It is a massive, impressive fortress—the largest in Europe. Before you absorb the detail of the treasures beyond the walls of La Cité, view it from the banks of the River **Aude**—the perspective you see will set the scene perfectly for your walking efforts to come. It is said Viollet-le-Duc used a bit too much imagination (as he did at Pierrefonds) in his restoration work; perhaps—but you will be lacking in imagination if your senses fail to be aroused by this majestic fortress from the past.

Briançon is the highest town in Europe. Above the modern town is the Ville Haute and a citadel—designed by Vauban—with three rows of ramparts. The Grande Rue in the Ville Haute is full of medieval treasures; the views from the ramparts and the citadel are extensive and inspiring, surrounded as you are by high mountains above you and the River **Durance** far below.

Embrun is south of Briançon and it, too, sits above the Durance. Once it was an important fortified town and ecclesiastical centre; its church is probably the finest in the Dauphiny Alps. Forests, rivers, streams, mountains, lakes and high Alpine passes encircle the small town—you can never get bored in places like this and, what is more, you will have the neighbouring countryside to yourself!

Montreuil-sur-Mer, its full name, was once a port; but the **Canche** long ago silted up and now it sits 10 kilometres inland. Its history goes back to Roman times but its main importance came in the 13th and 14th centuries. Victor Hugo, in *Les Miserables*, and Sterne, in *A Sentimental Journey*, both wrote of it; for me its special pleasure is the ramparts. Don't be faint-hearted about it; do the whole circuit.

Pérouges has intrigued my wife and me for over two decades. Four centuries ago it was a busy place; three centuries later it had all but disappeared. The last 50 years have seen it completely restored. It is the most perfect of all the fortified towns; although hardly a *town* now—just a village. Nothing clashes; nothing jars the eye. We always try to see it at dusk before visiting one of the great Ain restaurants—the twilight enhances its fine setting and makes it easier to visualise its busy life all those centuries ago. Don't bypass *Les Dombes*—the fine countryside to the north-west, peppered with hundreds of lakes.

Aigues-Mortes—once a port—has long since been left behind by the Mediterranean; from the ramparts of this astonishing fortress the blue sea can be seen a few kilometres to the south. There was a village here in Roman times but it was Saint Louis, at the time of his Crusades, who gave it importance. He built the circular keep, the Tour de Constance, with its five metres thick walls. His son, Philip the Bold, organised the building of the walls, towers and gates. The Camargue lies to the east, another attraction of this southern part of France.

Entrevaux is a fine example of how important a small fortified town like this must have been centuries ago. It is entered by a narrow bridge over the **Var**—ramparts surround it and a citadel sits high above the town. It was strengthened by Vauban and it is not difficult to see why it had such military importance.

There are dozens of *bastides* (fortified towns) in the south-west corner of France. All of them were built 700 to 800 years ago by both the Kings of England and of France. They all have a common design: rectangular in shape with fortified walls, and streets —within the walls—which all run at right-angles to each other. In the centre is a fortified church and, nearby, a main square with covered arcades. The best examples are between the River Lot and the River Dordogne: **Monpazier** (built by the English) and **Villeréal** (built by the French).

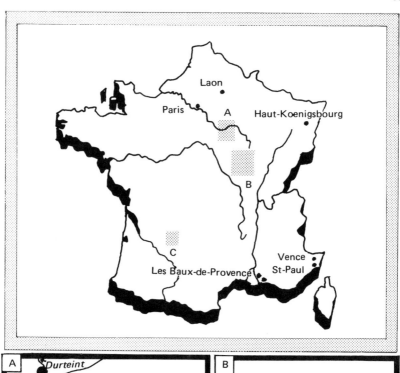

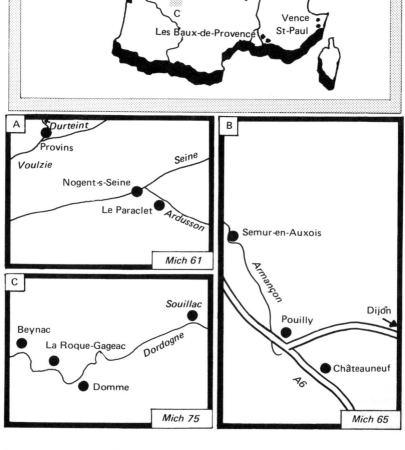

As I start many of these short chapters, I realise that one page is hardly enough to do justice to the topic at hand: this section is a classic example. There are scores of places, throughout France, that could be included here. I have incorporated many of the missing ones into other chapters; those that follow are just a few examples of this particular type of *treasure*, with which France is so richly endowed.

Laon was once the capital of France; it sits majestically on a solitary hill, towering above the surrounding country. One of the finest cathedrals in France is its centrepiece —but any walk through this hilltop town will return many benefits; ancient houses in old streets, and extensive views are always at hand.

Provins is a town unknown to most tourists. Its site does not lie on any of the recognised north–south routes and few travellers pass it on the east–west road; as a consequence they all miss this intriguing old place. The huge ramparts, built by the English during the Hundred Years War, are still there. To the north is Champagne country; to the south is a steep slope bordered by the **Durteint** and **Voulzie** streams: to the east is the Church of St-Ayoul, where Abelard once taught. South-east of Provins, 7 kilometres beyond **Nogent-s-Seine**, on the D442, are the ruins of **Le Paraclet** alongside the **Ardusson**. This was the hermitage to which Abelard was banished; when he left it he gave it to Heloïse, who became the Abbess there. Their story has become immortalised; Abelard died at Cluny but was buried at Le Paraclet. Now the two of them are buried together in the Père Lachaise Cemetery in **Paris**. In that cemetery lie Marshal Ney, Balzac, Bizet, Colette, Chopin, Molière, Proust, Oscar Wilde, Sarah Bernhardt and Edith Piaf.

Haut-Kœnigsbourg is a fantastic castle, perched like an eagle, high in the Vosges; it overlooks the vast plain of Alsace, the Rhine and the Black Forest, far to the east. It was restored in 1900 by Kaiser Wilhelm II; a marvellous place for adults and children alike —a Grimm's fairy-tale castle if ever there was one!

The River **Armançon** *loops* in a circle around the massive walls of the old Burgundian town of **Semur-en-Auxois**—making it into all but an island. Gigantic towers, precipitous views, tree-lined avenues, verdant countryside—it has everything. This is the real Burgundy—the same now as it was centuries ago.

Châteauneuf. How many of you have motored down the A6 and, just south of the exit for **Pouilly** and **Dijon**, admired the small fortified village perched high above the autoroute to the left? Next time, instead of sitting there admiring it, think how nice it would be to see it. Leave at the exit for Pouilly and explore this tiny place; only recently has some of it been restored by individuals, with Government financial aid—but much remains to be done. Châteauneuf is the Burgundian equivalent of the numerous *perched* villages in Provence and the Côte d'Azur.

Les Baux-de-Provence is a haunting, ghost-ridden village, *perched* on a hilltop in the Chaîne des Alpilles—the strangest outcrop of hills in France. Over 300 years ago it was a flourishing place; Louis XIII was the individual who ordered the town destroyed. It gave its name to Bauxite, discovered hereabouts.

St-Paul is one of the *jewels* of the Côte d'Azur with attractive, narrow streets, full of old houses and mountains. Don't miss the ramparts and the extensive views on all sides—mountains to the north and the shimmering Mediterranean to the south.

Vence is five kilometres to the north of St-Paul. Now it has a new town, surrounded by slopes with numerous villas and flats; but it is the old walled town that attracts me, especially the Romanesque cathedral with its fine choir stalls.

Domme lies immediately to the south of the **Dordogne** and high above that lovely river. It, too, is a *bastide*—but its shape has been adapted to suit the contours of the rocky hill. Don't miss nearby **Beynac** and **La Roque-Gageac**.

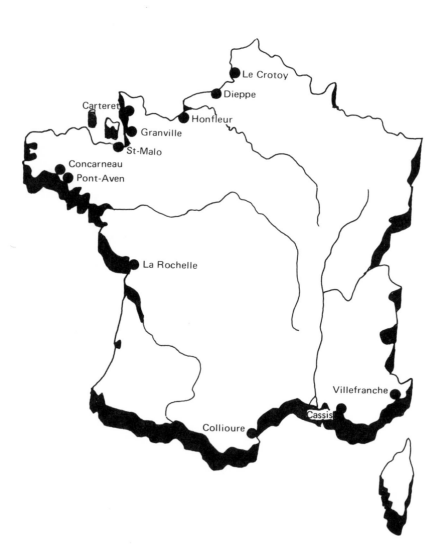

Le Crotoy
Dieppe
Carteret
Honfleur
Granville
St-Malo
Concarneau
Pont-Aven
La Rochelle
Villefranche
Cassis
Collioure

PORTS

I hope I do not offend some people who love France in omitting—inevitably—some of their favourite ports. I have chosen to highlight just twelve of them—varying from the tiniest fishing ports to bustling, busy ones where all types of shipping ply back and forth crossing the oceans of the world.

Any permutation of the twelve, however, will provide you with enough evidence to support my view that ports are amongst the most interesting of villages and towns; active, full of life and with a special character inland places cannot emulate. I'll describe my favourite twelve, in anticlockwise order, starting in the far north.

Le Crotoy must be the tiniest of the twelve. It sits at the mouth of the Somme with wide open beaches stretching far to the north. Children will have the place to themselves—you will have little else to do but join them in the fun of exploring the mud flats and beaches. Only a few fishing boats use the place—try to enjoy some of their catches, plucked from the sea, at the local restaurants.

Dieppe is quite different. It has its sad reminders of the last war—particularly the tragic 1942 Commando raid made by Canadian and Scottish troops; but today, particularly on Saturdays, (when its streets become one big, open-air market) it is a happy place—full of the produce of the sea and the Normandy hinterland.

Honfleur is a paradise for artists. It is full of old houses, the lovely Ste-Catherine's Church, an old dock and plenty of varied craft in its harbour.

The western edge of the Cotentin Peninsula has several gems in its collection of treasures. The working harbours of **Carteret** and **Granville**—the latter has fine ramparts and rocks as an added bonus—are the best examples on this coastline.

Brittany has more examples of colourful ports than the rest of France put together. **St-Malo**, badly damaged during the last war, will please young and old alike: ramparts, an old town, an amazing amount of river and sea-traffic, are all at hand.

Southern Brittany has two special favourite ports of mine; **Concarneau** is both a very busy fishing port and an old town enclosed within granite walls and ramparts. The harbour, nearby beaches and a Fishing Museum will provide you with hours of entertainment. **Pont-Aven** is an *inland* port: full of old mills, long since converted; here, mimosa and palm trees thrive alongside each other. No wonder so many painters were inspired at Pont-Aven—Gauguin was the most famous amongst them.

Far to the south is **La Rochelle**—for so long the gateway to the New World of North America. History flows through the very soul of this thriving port—you feel it as you walk the streets and quaysides. It is renowned for its marvellous light. The town, with its massive towers, is at its best in the early evening; later you can admire the really clever use made of street lighting—lamps are mounted on the tops of buildings—to illuminate the old port and quaysides.

Of my three Mediterranean selections, **Collioure** is the most southern of them —close to the Spanish border. It is an impressive site—loved by painters—with beaches, a harbour and a medieval fort. With the Pyrénées on one side, and the blue sea on the other, what more could you want? In spring Collioure is at its best; a mass of flowers and colour everywhere—camellias, wistaria, roses and fruit blossom.

Cassis is my next choice. No fort here but it is even more picturesque than Collioure. Lovely plane trees, fountains and Cassis wines are all there to add to its other ancient attractions. It, too, has spectacular coastlines to both sides, and inland are many tranquil villages, basking in the hot, scorching Provençal sun.

Villefranche is the last of my twelve favourite ports. Its deep harbour is a safe anchorage for visiting ocean-going cruise ships and naval warships from all corners of the world. Full of old streets, it has mountains rearing high above it; and across the water is the fine sight of wooded Cap Ferrat.

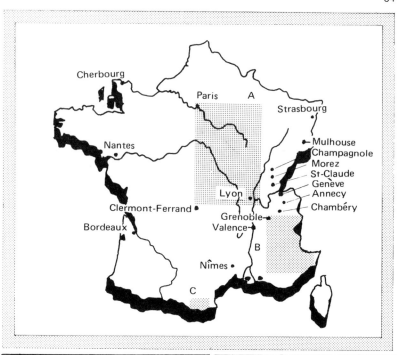

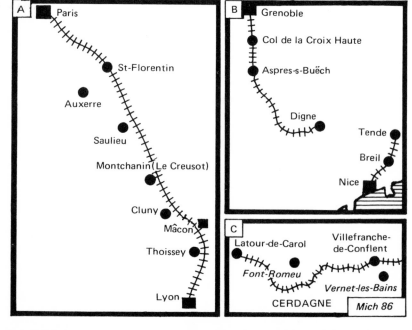

RAILWAYS—STATE-OWNED

Enthusiasts, children and—dare I say it—all adults, will find dozens of opportunities, throughout France, of savouring the best parts of both the state-owned railway system and of the many privately-owned lines. The state-owned railways are second to none; the private ones, with one or two exceptions, do not match some of the more enterprising private lines in the U.K.

I can only highlight a few of the possibilities—spread throughout the country.

The French Railway Museum at **Mulhouse** is worth a long detour for any visitor to eastern France; it is open daily throughout the year. There are dozens of locomotives, coaches and other interesting rolling stock set out on six tracks.

French Railways have made tremendous progress in the use of electric locomotives and, more recently, in the introduction of gas turbine *turbotrains*; these are used on the major express lines and, in scaled-down form, on many minor lines. Much the most exciting development has been the building of a completely new line from **Paris** to **Lyon** to take the new TGV (*Train à Grande Vitesse*—very high speed) trains of the future. These will operate at 260/300 kilometres per hour—the journey time from Paris to Lyon will be just two hours! In early 1981 a speed of 380 k.p.h (236 m.p.h.) was attained on this track—a world speed record.

The track has been carefully planned. Because of shock waves as two trains pass each other, the twin tracks are some 5 metres apart and sharp curves have been completely avoided, only one curve having a tighter radius than four kilometres. The track can be inspected at many points: south-east of **Saulieu** (use the N6 at the point where it crosses over the new line—a staggering experience); north of **Cluny**; east of **Thoissey**. Better still, in late 1981, the first operating section will open—from **St-Florentin** (north-east of **Auxerre**) to Lyon. Two new stations will be opened at the same time; at **Mâcon** and at **Montchanin** (**Le Creusot**). Soon I will be parking my car at one of those stations and trying a short, fast, high-speed journey!

French Railways have been using *turbotrains* for over 10 years. There are two main types. The ETG (using an aeronautical gas turbine engine—with a diesel engine fitted as a secondary power unit) was the first to be used; today, it still runs on the **Lyon–Grenoble**, **Lyon–Chambery/Annecy** and **Valence–Genève** lines. The RTG (a second generation *turbotrain*—it has the diesel engine removed) has two turbo-engines capable of moving the train at 200 kilometres per hour. These units cover the **Paris–Cherbourg**, **Lyon–Strasbourg**, **Lyon–Nantes** and **Lyon–Bordeaux** routes. They provide the same performance as electrified locomotives—but, of course, there are none of the high costs of laying down electric lines.

Here are some other ideas for scenic enjoyment.

In the Jura use the minor line from **Champagnole** to **St-Claude**. The tunnels and viaducts at **Morez** are particularly interesting.

The line from **Grenoble** to **Digne**—and particularly the section across the **Col de la Croix Haute**—is a spectacular one, full of technical ingenuity. A return run from **Grenoble** to **Aspres-s-Buëch** would be an enjoyable way to spend a scenically rewarding day (in winter it is a specially exciting run).

The same is true of the line from **Nice** to **Breil** and **Tende** (north-east of Nice).

In the Massif Central the main line from **Clermont-Ferrand** to **Nîmes**, and a score of minor lines, will give endless opportunities to see the attractive countryside.

In the far south one very spectacular run is on *La Voie Métrique* from **Villefranche-de-Conflent** (alt. 427m) climbing high into the **Cerdagne** (the highest point reached is 1592m) and finishing at **Latour-de-Carol**; a total distance of 62 kilometres. Try to find a place in an open car *(la barque)* on this unusual train—called the *Canari*, because of its red and yellow livery!

66

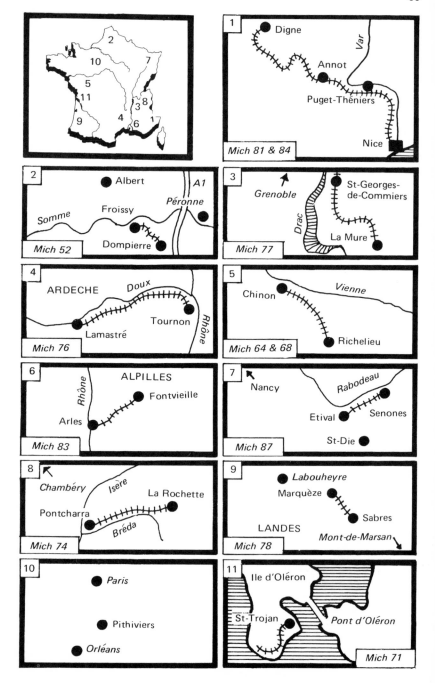

RAILWAYS—PRIVATELY-OWNED

During the last decade there has been a steady growth of interest throughout France in reviving old railway lines. Dozens of privately-owned systems are there to be enjoyed: a number of them have steam-driven engines—unfortunately, many are only open at weekends. I have given you as much information as I can but I do urge you to check opening times with French Railways at 179 Piccadilly, London W1 or the Tourist Offices in your country—page 144. Better still, enquire locally.

Chemins de Fer de Provence (1). This is an important and major link between **Digne** and **Nice**. Diesel cars ply this metric gauge line; all of it is spectacular, scenically exciting and full of technical interest. During 1980 an old steamer was revived to do the short hop between **Annot–Puget-Théniers**, using the same track as the Digne–Nice line; it was given the charming name *Train des Pignes* (Pines). During the first two seasons it was available to groups only, but by 1982 this steam run should be available to all—let's hope so.

Chemin de Fer Touristique Froissy–Dompierre (2). A short seven kilometres run on 60 cm. track. South of the River **Somme**, just west of the A1 Autoroute and south of **Albert**; steamers only on Sundays and fête days during the summer—see diesels running on Wednesdays and Saturdays from mid-July to end-August.

Chemin de Fer de Saint-Georges-de-Commiers à La Mure (3). A truly astonishing 30 kilometres run, full of exciting sections. It starts at the SNCF connecting station at St-Georges and then, as a *voie métrique*, it winds its way up to La Mure. Unhappily it only runs on Sundays from June–September.

Chemin de Fer du Vivarais (4). Don't miss this on any account; it is my favourite —only bettered by the superb Festiniog line in Wales. A metre gauge run of 33 kilometres from **Tournon** (where it shares the SNCF station), following the **Doux** Valley on its climb of 250 metres to **Lamastre**. This is **Ardèche** country—a delightful part of France: you, not to mention your children, are missing a real treat if you pass by this little gem of a trip on your mad dash south. You will never find the real, hidden France if you commit that sin. It runs every day in June, July and August; Saturday and Sunday in September and Sundays only in October. Both steam and diesel trains operate on this line—used by both locals and visitors.

Chemin de Fer Touristique Chinon–Richelieu (5). A 20 kilometres run on standard gauge track; Saturdays and Sundays from mid-June to mid-September. A steam and autorail line surrounded by lovely country, full of historical interest.

Chemin de Fer Touristique des Alpilles (6). From the SNCF station at **Arles**, this short steam run of nine kilometres takes you to **Fontvieille**; Sundays only from end-June to mid-September. Nothing spectacular about this one.

Chemin de Fer Touristique de la Vallée du Rabodeau (7). From **Senones** to **Etival**, the latter on the line from **Nancy** to **St-Die**; a 10 kilometres steam line open on every Saturday and Sunday in June, July and August; in April, May and September— every fortnight. In the middle of fine Vosges country.

Chemin de Fer Touristique du Bréda (8). A standard gauge line from **Pontcharra**, in the **Isère** Valley, through the **Gorges du Bréda**, to **La Rochette**. Steam trains run from June to September; enquire locally for days and times of operation.

Chemin de Fer Touristique des Landes de Gascogne (9). Steam trains run on Sundays and fête days (March to November) from **Sabres** to **Marquèze**, where there is a fine ecological museum deep in the heart of the **Landes** forests.

Musée des Transports de Pithiviers (10). A museum, full of old rolling stock and a short 60 cm. gauge line; the latter is open on Sundays (May–October).

Tramway Touristique de St-Trojan (11). On the **Ile d'Oléron**, at the mainland bridge. A six kilometres, 60 cm. gauge run—from Easter to September (daily).

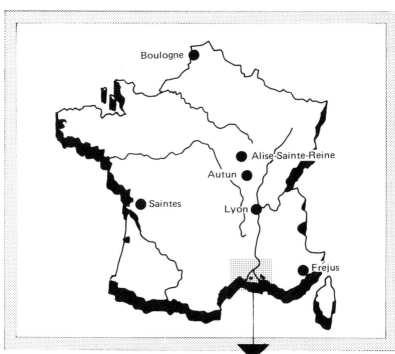

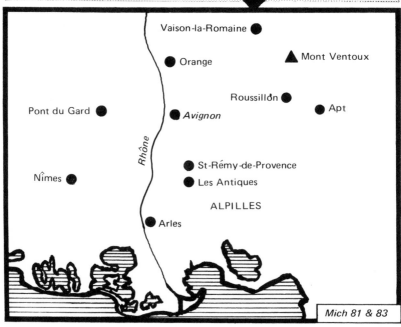

Mich 81 & 83

Most visitors to France will associate its Roman history with Provence; they are right to do this—many of my suggestions set down on this page highlight the Provençal treasures—but others throughout France should also be considered.

Burgundy has two Roman sites worth a detour.

The first is at **Alise-Sainte-Reine**. The Alise part of the name comes from *Alesia*, of Gallic fame; it was in these placid Burgundian hills that Julius Caesar won his famous seige victory over Vercingétorix, the commander of the Gauls.

Autun was called the *sister of Rome* by Julius Caesar. In the time of Augustus it was a flourishing place on the road from **Lyon** to **Boulogne**. Its Roman theatre—now in ruins—could hold 15000 spectators; still to be seen in Autun are two well-preserved Roman gates. The town has other highlights; the Cathedral of Saint-Lazare, with its magnificent tympanum of the Last Judgement, and the Musée Rolin.

Saintes, once the capital of Western Gaul, has many treasures from Roman to Romanesque. Of the Roman ones, there is a finely preserved arch dedicated to Germanicus, the Emperor Tiberius and his son Drusus. The ruins of what was a vast Roman arena (capable of holding 20000 spectators) lies to the west of the town.

The many Roman splendours of Provence could enthrall you for days on end.

Arles is my favourite Provençal town. The amphitheatre could seat 21000 people—and it is older than the Colosseum in Rome. The Roman theatre should be next on your list; its stage is the same width as the floor of the arena at Arles.

Vaison-la-Romaine is my favourite small town in Provence—a small-scale Pompeii. Magnificent finds have been made over the years; there are two areas to explore, the Puymin Quarter and the Villasse Quarter. Both contain streets, houses and fountains; there is a Roman theatre and a museum full of precious objects. Vaison has a splendid setting with **Mont Ventoux** as a spectacular backcloth.

Nîmes is the rival of Arles. It, too, has a huge, well-preserved amphitheatre and the Maison Carrée; a magnificent temple—or square house—Roman designed and built but very much in the Greek style. Don't miss the Jardin de la Fontaine, created 200 years ago on the site of the ruins of the old Roman baths.

Orange has its own famous triumphal arch—built to celebrate Caesar's victory over Pompey and the exploits of the 11th Legion. The Roman theatre is the greater treasure; the best-preserved and finest in existence today.

Pont du Gard is one of the wonders of the world. The aqueduct and bridge were constructed 2000 years ago and are marvels in every sense; in engineering and architectural terms, and in their site. It is best seen in the cool of the evening; it seems an even greater miracle of the Roman times in the twilight. An extra bonus at that hour is that the crowds have gone!

Apt is known for its flourishing fruit, preserves and crystallised fruit industries. The town has an interesting Archaeological Museum and, to the west, the Pont Julien, an old Roman bridge. Visit the ochre hills to the north-west and see how the varying shades of rock have been used to build the houses at **Roussillon**.

Fréjus is to the east of Provence. It was founded by Julius Caesar and developed as a port by Augustus, though the sea is some distance away these days. The town is full of Roman interests: an arena, a theatre and an aqueduct are amongst them.

St-Rémy-de-Provence lies to the north of the **Alpilles**. Between those hills and the town are the old Roman ruins called **Les Antiques**. This was once the prosperous town of Glanum. Several interesting parts still remain; amongst them a splendid triumphal arch and a first century mausoleum, built as a memorial to the grandsons of Emperor Augustus. Put aside an hour or so to explore the excavations at Glanum—they are full of interest; temples, baths and a forum amongst them.

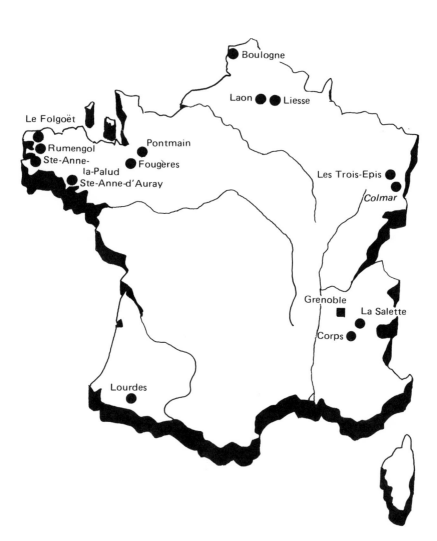

Boulogne

Laon ● ● Liesse

Le Folgoët
● Rumengol
Ste-Anne-
la-Palud
● Ste-Anne-d'Auray

Pontmain
● Fougères

Les Trois-Epis ●
Colmar

Grenoble
■ La Salette
Corps ●

Lourdes

SHRINES

Many Catholics—from all corners of the world—make pilgrimages to the Shrines of France: Catholics or not, all of us can gain inspiration from our own visits to these sites. I list some of the most important ones.

La Salette. High above **Corps**, at an altitude of 1770 metres, is the Romanesque-style Basilica, made of black marble. Corps lies on the Route Napoléon (page 47) 65 kilometres south of **Grenoble**. At this remote spot on September 19, 1846, the Virgin Mary appeared to two small children from Corps while they protected their sheep on the mountain pastures. Within a few years the Vision was authenticated—by 1861 the Basilica had been finished. It is a marvellous, inspiring site.

Lourdes. On Thursday, February 11, 1858, a young 14 year old girl was collecting wood by the Gave (a river); the Virgin Mary appeared in a grotto of the Massabielle Rock and spoke to the child, Bernadette Soubirous. During the next five months there were no fewer than 18 appearances and a spring broke through at a spot the Virgin had indicated to her. "I am the Immaculate Conception," said the Virgin—words the small girl did not understand but she repeated them to herself time after time in case she forgot them. A chapel was built at the spring and what has happened in the 120 years since is now common knowledge.

Pontmain. Leave **Fougères** to the north on the D177—pass through the Forêt de Fougères (worth a short exploration) and then, at Landéan, strike north-east, on the D19 to Pontmain. Eugène Barbedette first saw the vision on January 17, 1871; his father, when called, could not see the shining lady—his brother, Joseph, could. None of the adults, nuns included, saw the vision—but all the village children, however young, did so. The message given was; "Pray my children. God will soon grant your prayers." Eleven days later the Franco-Prussian War finished—an armistice was signed. A Basilica was built on the spot at the end of the 19th century.

Pilgrimages are made to many other spots in France—to a hundred or more. Amongst the most important are:

Boulogne, where watchmen at the port saw the Virgin Mary in 636. For centuries Boulogne was as important a centre of pilgrimage as Lourdes is today.

Liesse is 12 kilometres east of that splendid hilltop town of **Laon**, once the capital of France. The Basilica here was built on the spot where, on July 2, 1134, three Knights of St-John, together with the Saracen Princess Ismeria, woke by the side of a fountain after their long trek back from a Crusade in Egypt where they had been fighting the Saracens. For a time the Knights had been imprisoned in a Saracen prison where they had miraculously found an effigy; this had been the cause of the conversion of Ismeria. At Liesse it mysteriously became too heavy to carry and this they took as a sign to build a chapel for it. Kings, Queens and Saints have made the pilgrimage to Our Lady of Liesse.

Les Trois-Epis. On May 3, 1491, the Virgin appeared to Théodore Schoeré at a lonely spot where a man had been killed; he was praying there for the dead man's soul to be saved. In one hand the Virgin held an icicle (the punishment of sins) and in the other, three ears of corn (the reward for penitence). A chapel was built on the spot and the village took its name from those three ears of corn.

All visitors to Brittany should try to see one of the Breton *pardons*. Some of these have continued unbroken for a thousand years. The procession which takes place first, in the afternoon, provides the rare chance to see the lovely Breton costumes and head-dresses. After the procession everyone enjoys themselves at a fair. Some of the most famous *pardons* are at:

Le Folgoët—*Grand Pardon* on the 1st Sunday in September; **Ste-Anne-la-Palud**—*Grand Pardon* on the 1st Sunday after August 15; **Ste-Anne-d'Auray**—*Grand Pardon* on July 26; **Rumengol**—*Pardon* on Trinity Sunday.

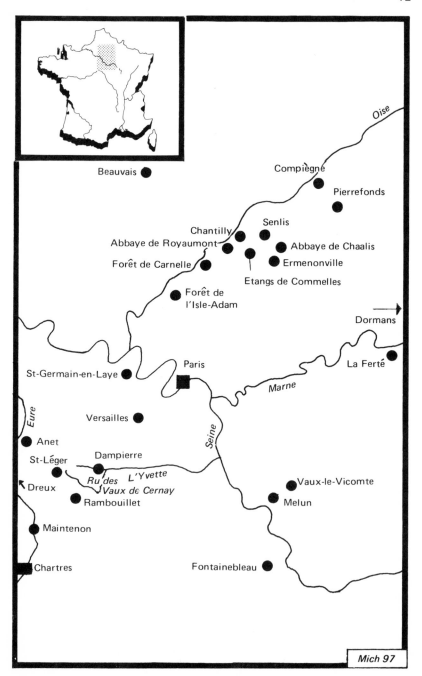

Beauvais

Oise

Compiègne

Pierrefonds

Senlis

Chantilly

Abbaye de Royaumont

Abbaye de Chaalis

Forêt de Carnelle

Ermenonville

Etangs de Commelles

Forêt de
l'Isle-Adam

Dormans

Paris

St-Germain-en-Laye

La Ferté

Marne

Eure

Versailles

Seine

Anet

St-Léger

Dampierre

Vaux-le-Vicomte

Ru des L'Yvette

Dreux

Vaux de Cernay

Melun

Rambouillet

Maintenon

Chartres

Fontainebleau

Mich 97

This green, wooded *island* surrounds **Paris**: it is full of treasures. The forests of **St-Germain-en-Laye**, **Compiègne** and **Fontainebleau** are mentioned elsewhere; but other forests worth exploring are at **Chantilly**, **Ermenonville** and **Rambouillet**.

The cathedrals at **Beauvais** and **Chartres** are described in another part of this book—as, indeed, are the palaces at **Fontainebleau** and **St-Germain-en-Laye**. What are some of the other treasures and attractions—both architectural and natural—that you must seek out as you travel across this part of France?

All the country lying in the rough triangle from **St-Léger** to **Rambouillet** and **Dampierre** is superb: extensive woods with several small lakes and streams running through them—the best of the latter are the delightfully named **Ru des Vaux de Cernay** and **L'Yvette**. Dampierre and Rambouillet have their own elegant châteaux.

The **Eure** Valley, running north from Chartres to **Dreux** and **Anet** (each of the three with their own *pearls*) handsomely repays the effort needed to seek it out and follow the roads along its banks. A bonus on this diversion is the beautifully situated château at **Maintenon**. An attractive park and gardens are its highlights—designed by that master gardener Lenôtre; his name appears regularly in this book.

On the north-west side of Paris the same thing can be said of the **Marne** Valley—or should I say the 30 or 40 kilometres upstream from **La Ferté** to **Dormans**.

Of the man-made sites, there are many which are worth a long diversion. This book, written for the motorist, ignores Paris; but you could spend many days doing justice to the Ile de France alone, as it contains so many captivating delights.

Versailles and its colossal, majestic palace is the most famous of the treasures. It is definitely not a place to *do* just once; you could make several visits over the years and still not absorb all its priceless wonders. There are the various superb apartments; the extensive and famous gardens (250 acres of them) and the Trianons (the Grand Trianon has been lavishly restored by the Government so that visiting Heads of State can stay there).

On the south-east side of Paris is the château at **Vaux-le-Vicomte** (near **Melun**) —another huge and magnificent structure, built just before Versailles.

Chantilly is famous for many reasons: its racecourse, its forests and its château. But if, like me, your main loves are the outdoor pleasures of life, don't miss the walks in the woods encircling the **Etangs de Commelles** (south of Chantilly).

To the west of these *etangs* is the 700 year old **Abbaye de Royaumont**; another of the many *children* of Cîteaux. Even today, it manages to demonstrate what an impressive place it must have been at the peak of its influence. Nearby is the **Oise** Valley and, as it flows towards the **Seine**, on its southern banks, are two smaller stretches of forest: the **Forêt de Carnelle** and the **Forêt de l'Isle-Adam**. All this northern loop of country is at its best in the spring or the autumn.

Autoroutes are useful but they are a temptation for the modern generation: they entice you past so many of the historical pleasures of France. **Senlis** is a perfect example: a quiet and calm place with a cathedral whose construction commenced in 1153. It is full of medieval houses, monuments and Gallo-Roman remains.

One treasure that appeals to my heart and eyes is the **Abbaye de Chaalis**—founded in 1136 but now in ruins and amid charming gardens and woods; the nearby Parc d'Ermenonville is surrounded by the forest of the same name.

Finally, there remain two essential ports of call in the north-east corner of the region: the immense Palace of **Compiègne**; and the awesome castle at **Pierrefonds**, which Viollet-le-Duc restored and, like another of his masterpieces—the fortress at Carcassonne—it is said the final result of his work represents more of what he thought it should have looked like, than a precise reproduction.

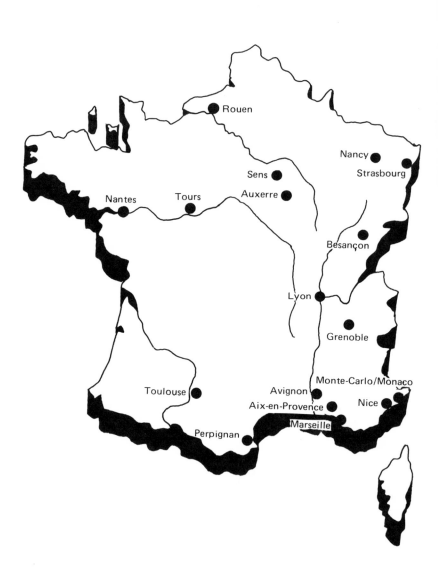

Rouen

Nancy

Strasbourg

Sens

Auxerre

Nantes   Tours

Besançon

Lyon

Grenoble

Monte-Carlo/Monaco

Toulouse

Avignon

Aix-en-Provence   Nice

Marseille

Perpignan

TREASURES OF THE TOWNS

The prime objective of this small book is to highlight the special attractions of provincial and rural France; a car is an essential prerequisite for you to find them. Aided by the many maps, you will find no problems in identifying just where they are and then in reaching them, helped by large-scale maps.

The cities and towns of France have been both described and praised by countless guides. It is difficult for the independent motorist to enjoy the *treasures* of the towns: navigating there, parking, noise—all these headaches confront him.

Most of the travel and touring experiences of my childhood and teens were to the cities of this world: for the last 25 years I have enjoyed other pleasures. However, many of the treasures in the big cities and towns require you to put up with those headaches: some of the best sights are identified elsewhere in these pages; cathedrals, museums and so on. But other treasures exist—all worth the effort to find and enjoy. I will list some of my favourites in brief note form: try to see them when you are passing through or holidaying anywhere near these towns.

Côte d'Azur.
    Monte-Carlo/Monaco. The Jardin exotique. The Palais. The Oceanographic Museum and Aquarium. The Casino and its gardens.
    Nice. The Promenade des Anglais. The Flower Market. Several museums; particularly the National Museum with its *treasure chest* of Marc Chagall's work.

Provence.
    Marseille. Old Port. The Basilique Notre-Dame-de-la-Garde. The coast road south from the Old Port—the Corniche Prés. J. F. Kennedy.
    Avignon. The Palais des Papes and the gardens just north of them—the Rocher des Doms. Ramparts. The world-famous bridge—Pont St-Bénézet.
    Aix-en-Provence. The new autoroutes take you past this lovely place too easily. The old central area. The Cours Mirabeau. Several museums and churches.

Languedoc-Roussillon.
    Toulouse. Central and Vieux Toulouse. The Basilique St-Sernin. The Church of Les Jacobins. Several museums.
    Perpignan. The area south of the River Basse, before it enters the Têt.

Champagne-Ardenne.
    Nancy. Place Stanislas and all the area encircling it; full of museums and architectural treasures. Gardens—particularly La Pépinière.

Alsace.
    Strasbourg. Cathedral. Old Strasbourg. La Petit France. This is an old town which will entertain you for days on end—don't miss it.

Jura.
    Besançon. Its site on the River Doubs. Citadelle.

Hautes-Alpes.
    Grenoble. The Fort de la Bastille (overlooking Grenoble and the River Isère).

Lyonnais.
    Lyon. Its site. Old Lyon (west of the Saône). Basilique N.D. de Fourvière.

Burgundy
    Sens and **Auxerre**. Their cathedrals.

Loire.
    Tours. Old Tours. Cathedral.

Brittany.
    Nantes. Château Ducal. Cathedral.

Normandy.
    Rouen. Old Town. Cathedral. Museums. Churches. Views—above the town.

76

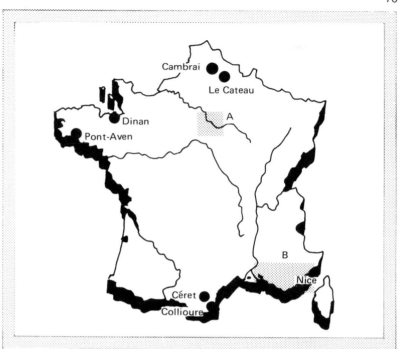

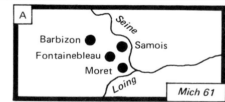

Barbizon
Samois
Fontainebleau
Moret
Seine
Loing

Mich 61

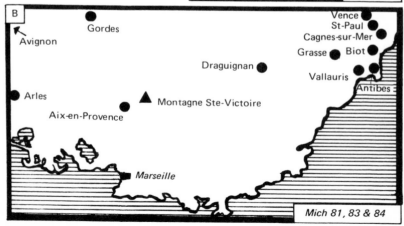

A

B

Vence
St-Paul
Cagnes-sur-Mer
Grasse · Biot
Vallauris
Antibes
Gordes
Avignon
Draguignan
Arles
Montagne Ste-Victoire
Aix-en-Provence
Marseille

Mich 81, 83 & 84

ARTISTS

One of the great interests in my life is to paint and draw: unhappily, lack of time has allowed me to do only a tiny amount of work during the last 25 years.

What I have been able to do during those years is to absorb the character, style, light and feel of many parts of France—famous for their scenes, so brilliantly captured by artists through the simple mediums of paint, pencil and ink. Where are some of these places in the many regions of France?

Most of them are in the south. The Côte d'Azur is the most richly endowed with the work of men who created their masterpieces in the brilliant light of the south. Auguste Renoir lived at **Cagnes-sur-Mer**; first at the Post Office, then at Les Colettes, the house in which he spent the last 12 years of his life. It is now a museum and is well worth a visit—don't roar past on the nearby autoroute.

Paul Cézanne used to visit Renoir at Les Colettes; he did all his work in the magical light of **Aix-en-Provence**. **Montagne St-Victoire**—to the east of the town—featured in dozens of his paintings: as you approach it you will recognise the mountain from those paintings, without the need to refer to any map or guide book!

Picasso did much of his work on the Côte d'Azur. The Musée Picasso, at the Château Grimaldi in **Antibes**, houses some of his best work; it includes all the paintings and ceramics he produced in the autumn of 1946 when he lived at the Château. At nearby Vallauris, the potters' town, made famous by Picasso, are clear signs of the influence he had on the development of ceramics and pottery skills.

The most famous of all the artists who did their work in Provence was Van Gogh—at **Arles**. The countryside surrounding the town, especially in spring, is alive with living reminders of the images this talented genius captured on canvas: flowers, trees, fields and houses. Any visitor to these parts will feel that same atmosphere.

Matisse did much of his superb work in the south. At **Nice** is the Matisse Museum: at **Vence** are his famous decorations at the Chapelle du Rosaire, just north of the town. Matisse was born at **Le Cateau**—far to the north, east of **Cambrai**; at weekends a museum there containing some of his work is open to the public. The National Museum at Nice houses some of Marc Chagall's best work.

There are many other museums in the south worth taking the time to search out. None are difficult to find and none present navigation problems in getting to them: there is the Fernand-Léger Museum at **Biot**; the Provençal Museum and the Maeght Foundation —both at **St-Paul**, south of **Vence**; two museums at **Grasse**; the Municipal Museum at **Draguignan**; a Vasarély exhibition at **Gordes**, east of **Avignon**.

At the other end of the French Mediterranean coast is the tiny town of **Céret**: modern painters have always had an affection for this corner of France; it houses a Musée d'Art Moderne, with works by Picasso, Matisse, Braque and Chagall. Nearby **Collioure** is a lovely spot; captured on canvas by Matisse and Braque.

The **Seine** and **Loing** rivers form the eastern and southern borders of the Forest of **Fontainebleau**. Sisley and Monet and many other Impressionist painters captured the scenes on these rivers and at the towns of **Samois** and **Moret**. **Barbizon**, in the forest, was made famous by the landscape painters of the 19th century—it still remains an attractive village—well worth a short diversion from the A6 Autoroute.

Brittany has its own association with many painters. **Pont-Aven** is the most famous of the many schools of painters: this small town inspired many, particularly Paul Gauguin. No wonder, as it is a glorious spot. Don't miss **Dinan** and the views of the Rance from the Jardin Anglais—a favourite subject of many artists.

Space has prevented me writing about other delightful places where artists have been inspired to do superb work. The same is true of musicians and writers; just a few have been mentioned in this book—perhaps later editions can do them justice.

I introduce the two chapters on the *Coastlines* of France by saying how favoured she has been by Nature; the same applies to her beaches—3000 kilometres of them!

They vary enormously. Some are vast, where low and high tides are hundreds of metres apart: others, particularly the Mediterranean ones, are narrow, tideless beaches. In August all are crowded; in the Med they are *sardine tins* with their oiled, topless occupants, lying jammed together. You may, or may not, find the thought of becoming a sardine yourself, irresistible—in the case of yours truly, although the imagination is willing, the old pilchard body would disqualify such nubile pleasure!

Let us do a tour, anticlockwise around France, of the possibilities open to you.

The North Sea washes the long, wide, sandy beaches on both sides of **Calais**. Our family have played many a game of football on them before catching ferries.

Wimereux is a drab place but it has fine beaches—similar to those south of **Le Touquet**. The latter has many other attractions for all the family.

The beaches of **Trouville** and **Deauville** are world famous. Similar pleasures of the type available at Le Touquet abound here: horse riding, tennis, swimming in magnificent pools, golf and the bonus of horse racing meetings. During the summer every imaginable type of gala and sporting event adds extra interest, colour and gaiety.

The west side of the **Cotentin** Peninsula is dotted with small resorts and working harbours; the tides have huge rises and falls and the beaches are vast.

The north Brittany coast changes character yet again. Just east of **St-Malo** are open beaches and rocky coves. **Dinard** is a family favourite: it has safe beaches, an Aquarium and a Maritime Museum. An added benefit is the large sea-water swimming pool—both our children learned, in a matter of days, how to swim in that *supporting* water. To the west are many small resorts and dozens of sandy coves.

At **Ste-Anne-la-Palud** is one of the best of all the Brittany beaches; secluded, vast and backed up by quiet countryside. The most famous of the southern beaches are those of **La Baule**, a fashionable resort just north of the **Loire**.

South of the Loire are many fine Atlantic beaches. **Les Sables-d'Olonne** is in the middle of this stretch—**Royan** at the end of it. The Islands of **Oléron** and **Ré** are described elsewhere—they provide interesting, quiet beach holidays.

South of the **Gironde** is the 150 kilometres long *beach* of the Landes. On gale-swept days the sight—and sound—of the Atlantic breakers rolling in is unforgettable.

The same magnificent sight is seen at its best at **Biarritz**. Like Deauville it presents every type of event during the season; there is marvellous countryside to the east. **St-Jean-de-Luz** is an alternative cheaper resort.

The Mediterranean scene is a world apart. At the southern end, near the Spanish border, are a series of resorts with sun-soaked beaches, backed by the Pyrénées—**Collioure** is my favourite. The new, man-made beaches, ports and resorts of Languedoc-Roussillon stretch in a huge silver arc to the Rhône delta: **St-Cyprien**, **Port-Barcarès** and **Port-Leucate** are amongst them. Buildings of the future, like white pyramids, line the Mediterranean at **La Grande-Motte**, near **Montpellier**. Not inspiring country but perfect for those looking for sun, sea and staying-put.

Finally, the beaches of Provence and the Riviera. As beaches go, apart from the other distractions mentioned earlier, they don't have much to offer! They are narrow and crowded (some are sandy, some stone)—but amongst them **Bandol**, **Le Lavandou**, **St-Tropez**, **Agay** and **Cannes** have provided us with fine, family holidays. Many other attractions combine to make this one of my favourite parts of France.

I have no doubt that I have probably not mentioned many a marvellous beach somewhere along that anticlockwise tour. But with 3000 kilometres of coast it would take a lifetime to explore all the many possibilities.

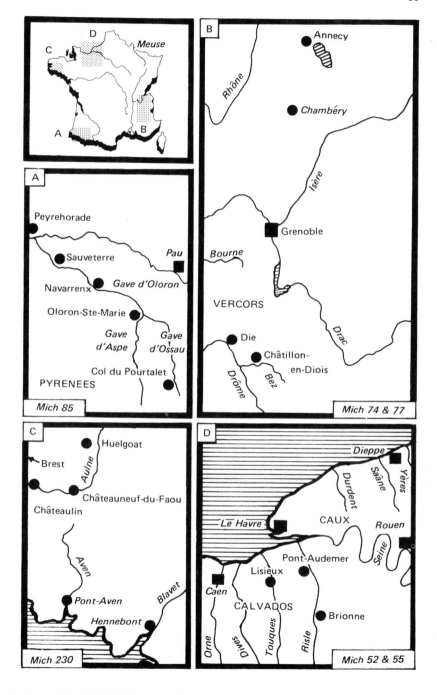

A

Peyrehorade

Sauveterre

Pau

Navarrenx

Gave d'Oloron

Oloron-Ste-Marie

Gave d'Aspe

Gave d'Ossau

Col du Pourtalet

PYRENEES

Mich 85

B

Rhône

Annecy

Chambéry

Isère

Grenoble

Bourne

VERCORS

Drac

Die

Châtillon-en-Diois

Drôme

Bez

Mich 74 & 77

C

Huelgoat

Brest

Aulne

Châteauneuf-du-Faou

Châteaulin

Aven

Blavet

Pont-Aven

Hennebont

Mich 230

D

Dieppe

Saâne

Durdent

Yères

Le Havre

CAUX

Rouen

Seine

Pont-Audemer

Lisieux

Brionne

Caen

CALVADOS

Orne

Dives

Touques

Risle

Mich 52 & 55

Meuse

C   D

A   B

FISHING

No fisherman am I: but I know the rivers of France particularly well. So, whether you are a serious participant, fishing to actually catch something, or one who is just happy to dabble and dally, content to sit against a tree and enjoy the unique pleasures of a French picnic and a water-cooled bottle of wine, or, the third sort of person, just pleased to lose yourself along river-banks—all of you will gain by making detours to the best streams in France. It is no coincidence that all the possibilities I highlight for you are set in gorgeous country and with fine, local cuisine as a bonus; some are in good wine-producing areas, too—there's more to fishing than catching fish!

Salmon fishing is at its best in the streams flowing down from the western **Pyrénées**. The most famous is the **Gave d'Oloron**, from **Peyrehorade** to **Sauveterre**, at its best in February and March. April and May see the next stretch at its best from Sauveterre to **Navarrenx**: the 40 kilometres upstream from the latter to **Oloron-Ste-Marie** are at their peak in June, July and August. This area of France is grand country; there are endless other pleasures to entice you—superb cuisine, inexpensive wines and Armagnac brandy from the hills to the north.

Trout fishing, too, in the Pyrénées is of an excellent standard—there are many streams providing good sport. Amongst the best trout and char streams is the **Gave d'Ossau** (a tributary of the Gave d'Oloron—running upstream from Oloron to its source, near the Spanish border at the **Col du Pourtalet**).

As popular as the Ossau is, the neighbouring **Gave d'Aspe** is even more highly thought of—it runs due south from Oloron-Ste-Marie and holds both char and trout.

In Brittany, far to the north, the best salmon fishing is found in the **Aulne**, that lovely estuary and river south-east of **Brest**. During the first three months of the year they are caught as far upstream as **Châteaulin**; from April to July the next section of the river, to **Châteauneuf-du-Faou**, is at its best; the upper stretch of the river provides the finest sport at the end of the season.

Trout, too, can be fished in the tributaries of the Aulne, and in the **Blavet** and the **Aven**; the streams and lakes near **Huelgoat** are renowned for trout, perch and carp. All these rivers and streams have good hotels in their vicinity.

Normandy is richly endowed with trout streams. In **Calvados** country are the **Orne**—best in its upper reaches; the **Dives**; the **Touques**—above **Lisieux**; and the **Risle**—from **Pont-Audemer** to **Brionne**. In **Caux** country, north of the **Seine**, are tiny streams like the **Yères**, the **Saâne** and the **Durdent**.

In the far north-east of France the **Meuse** and many of its tributaries offer some of the best trout fishing in Europe.

The Alps offer two differing types of sport; the mountain trout streams and the special treasures of the many lakes.

Of the streams and rivers, those of the Dauphiny Alps are particularly renowned. South of **Grenoble** is the **Drac**; to the west, in the **Vercors** Massif, is the **Bourne**, fed by many streams and with several reservoirs.

To the south of the Vercors, the upper reaches of the **Drôme** and one of its tributaries, the **Bez**, are both highly thought of: both **Die** (on the Drôme) and **Châtillon-en-Diois** (on the Bez) are renowned for their excellent wines—particularly the sparkling sort! What could be better than *local* wines cooled in *local* streams?

Of the many lakes in the French Alps, **Annecy** is perhaps the most rewarding. The lake yields *piscatorial treasures* unknown anywhere else in France. The menus of many restaurants in the region are built around these superb fish: salmon trout, some a metre long and weighing 15 kilograms; *omble chevalier*, the most subtle, and finest tasting of all freshwater fish (a char—it looks like a large salmon trout); *féra*; *lavaret*; *brochet* and *lotte* (a burbot, not unlike an eel).

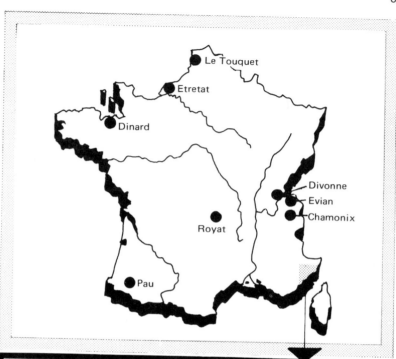

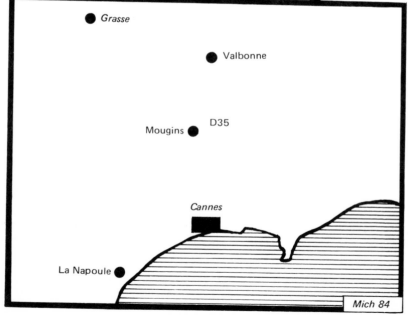

Mich 84

GOLFING

Even those readers addicted to the sport would probably not realise that one of the earliest golf courses to be opened anywhere in the world, outside Scotland, was in France—at **Pau**. After Blackheath and Calcutta, it was the third golf course to be built —it is much the oldest on the Continent.

I could not attempt to describe, on one page, all the fine courses in France. I list just a few of them, but they do all have some things in common: all are in fine countryside; all are excellent to play and all have that extra something that provides character and style to the course.

Pau was opened 125 years ago; and it was transformed into an 18-hole course by Sir Victor Brooke (father of Viscount Alanbrooke). It sits on the northern bank of the Gave de Pau—virtually a chip-shot away from the graceful town of Pau itself.

At the other end of the country are the many courses at **Le Touquet**. All of them are amongst the pine woods and sand dunes to the south of the resort. All of them have that special *air* of the seaside course.

Further down the coast, high above **Etretat** and its famous white cliffs, are the 18 holes of a most scenic course. Again, all the pleasure, and perils, of playing in the bracing air of seaside links await you here—but there is one unique difference: out-of-bounds it may be, but there is certainly no more magnificent *trap* anywhere in France— the huge white cliffs called the Falaise d'Aval.

West of **Dinard** and north of St-Briac-sur-Mer is the last of my *seaside specials*! The course has a marvellous setting—many of the best scenic aspects of the northern Brittany coast are on hand to put you off your shot at every tee.

A change of air now and away to the other side of France: to the lakes and mountains of the Jura and the Alps.

Divonne sits in the eastern shadow of the Jura; the Swiss frontier is a couple of kilometres away; Lake Geneva a little further. On the western side of this quiet, small spa town is a wooded, hilly course.

Evian is another spa town and is on the southern shores of Lake Geneva. In the green wooded hills above the town and lake is another lovely course. I suspect, once more, that you will be continually distracted by the scenic traps bewitching you at every turn; the countryside is at its best in the spring and autumn.

In the **Chamonix** Valley, under the shadow of the needle-like mountains called *Aiguilles* and the looming mass of Mont Blanc, is one of the most attractive nine-hole courses I know. I also know one French family who come to Chamonix twice every year: in February for the winter sports; in August for the summer pleasures. Dad plays golf, Mum and daughter play tennis and the young son swims to his heart's content.

On second thoughts, another nine-hole course that comes close to matching the Chamonix one is at **Royat**, in the Auvergne, high up in the wooded hills to the south of the town. It, too, has the bonus of being surrounded by so many scenic treasures. Other chapters in this book will give you a score or so of ideas to occupy your days here; for much of the year you will have the countryside to yourself.

My last selection is the 18-hole course on the D35, east of **Mougins**, on the incomparable Côte d'Azur. A sporting course has been hacked out of the forest—it is kept immaculate throughout the long hot and dry summer. Equally, the courses at **La Napoule** or at **Valbonne** could attract you; but whichever ones you choose it will be golf played and enjoyed in real style!

I hope I have given you enough in the way of information to persuade you to put your clubs in the back of the car. What could be nicer than enjoying all those special pleasures of France, with a round or two of your favourite sport thrown in for good measure? I can't think of a better combination.

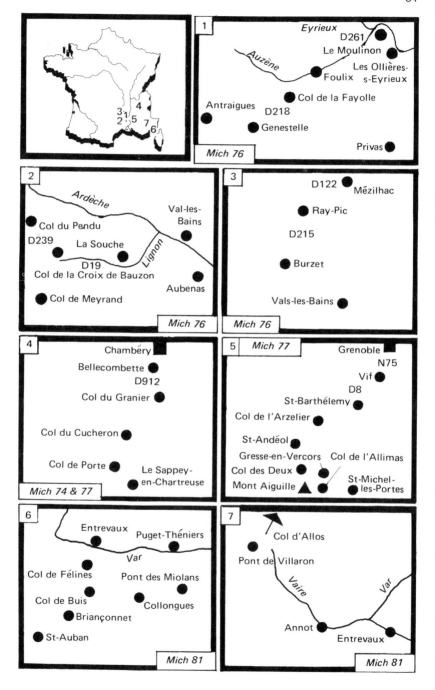

MONTE-CARLO RALLY COUNTRY

Most of you will have no interest whatever in motor sport: a few of you will be passionately interested—perhaps even competitors, past or present. All of you, with few exceptions, will be motorists and, hopefully, all of you are eager to see the scenic attractions that abound in France. I promise you all—whichever way you qualify—that any time you set aside in visiting the seven *stage* suggestions I list below will not be wasted.

The Monte-Carlo Rally is a January event: run, usually, on snow and ice in the best mountain country of Europe; terrain interlaced with thousands of minor roads. I have identified just a few of the many *stages* used in the Rally. The countryside surrounding them all also happens to be super scenic stuff—so seek them out.

You will be fascinated by just what the competing drivers and navigators, and their cars, have to cope with—usually on hard-packed snow and ice. You will be taking it easy, stopping frequently to admire a scenic aspect; they will be averaging speeds far in excess of anything you can safely do. Don't try to emulate them!

The stages are grouped into three areas of the south-east: the Ardèche; the Chartreuse and Vercors; and the Maritime Alps, between Digne and Grasse.

Ardèche. Michelin map 76—the south-east corner—will show you immediately just why this area is such interesting motoring country: it is a maze of mountain roads; and is at its best (for touring) in the spring and autumn.

Stage 1. Find **Privas** on map 76. North of the town is **Les Ollières-s-Eyrieux**. Two kilometres upstream on the River **Eyrieux** is **Le Moulinon**. Start here. Follow the **D261** up the **Auzène** Valley to **Foulix**. Climb up to the **Col de la Fayolle**. Then take the **D218** to **Genestelle** and finally **Antraigues**.

Stage 2. Find **Vals-les-Bains** and **Aubenas**. West of the latter in the **Lignon** Valley and on the **D19** is **La Souche**. Start here. Climb the **Col de la Croix de Bauzon**. At the **D239** turn north finishing after the **Col du Pendu**. Before you leave the area go south to the **Col de Meyrand**—magnificent panoramas await you.

Stage 3. Find **Burzet** (marvellous river scenery), north-west of **Vals-les-Bains**. Start here, using the **D215** to the north. Climb past the waterfall of **Ray-Pic**. At the **D122** turn right to finish at **Mézilhac**. A tremendous run—in every sense of the word.

Now across the Rhône to the **Chartreuse** (maps 74 and 77).

Stage 4. Take the **D912** south from Chambéry. The *stage* starts at **Bellecombette**. Climb the **Col du Granier**—keep going south. Climb the **Col du Cucheron** (map 77)—then the **Col de Porte**. Finish at **Le Sappey-en-Chartreuse**. This is glorious country—for me the best in France. Take your time; I certainly am not going to tell you the standard time allowed for this stage—it would turn your hair white!

Stage 5. Take the **N75** south of **Grenoble**. At **Vif** follow **D8** to **St-Barthélemy**. Start here: **Col de l'Arzelier**; **St-Andéol**; **Col des Deux**; **Gresse-en-Vercors**; **Col de l'Allimas**. In front of you is the most astonishingly-shaped mountain—**Mont Aiguille**. Keep your eyes on the road, or stop—and then admire it! Finish at **St-Michel-les-Portes**. This stage needs careful map reading.

The **Maritime Alps**. Amongst a dozen or so *stages* I list just two (map 81).

Stage 6. Find **Entrevaux** and **Puget-Théniers** in the **Var** Valley, north-west of Nice. In the hills to the south find **Pont des Miolans**. Start here. West to **Collongues**, **Briançonnet** and finish at **St-Auban**. Return to the Var Valley by going back on your tracks and then using the **Col de Buis** (I first found this *road* when the map showed it as a *footpath*) and the **Col de Félines**.

Stage 7. West of **Entrevaux** is **Annot**. Start here; climb the **Vaire** Valley, finishing at **Pont de Villaron**. Perhaps then you may have the appetite to try the **Col d'Allos**, to the north—an old favourite used years ago on the Alpine Rally.

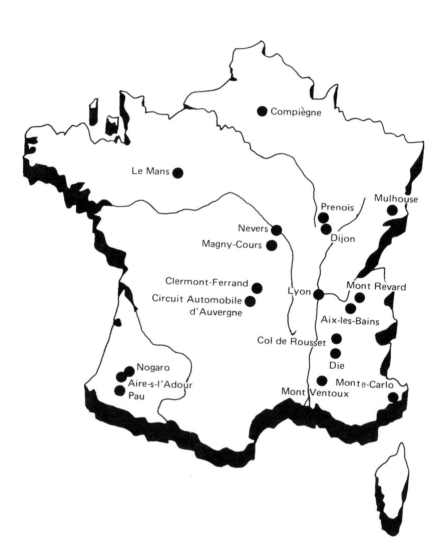

Compiègne

Le Mans

Prenois

Mulhouse

Nevers

Magny-Cours

Dijon

Clermont-Ferrand

Circuit Automobile
d'Auvergne

Lyon

Mont Revard

Aix-les-Bains

Col de Rousset

Nogaro

Aire-s-l'Adour

Pau

Die

Monte-Carlo

Mont Ventoux

MOTORING MEMENTOES

France—the birthplace of so much that has happened in motoring—is full of fascinating diversions for all motor sport enthusiasts. Your interests may be vintage or veteran cars, racing, hill climbing or visiting motor museums. I highlight just a dozen or so differing places, all easy to find and each of them worth a visit if you find yourself in the countryside nearby.

There are three major **Racing Circuits** well worth exploring—whether you are a motor sport fan or not. All of you will have watched racing at some time or other—there is no more dramatic way of discovering for yourself just how brave and skilful racing drivers are than by driving, sedately and safely, around these three circuits—all of which are open to you as they are normal public roads.

The most spectacular, attractive and breathtaking is the **Circuit Automobile d'Auvergne**; in the hills to the south-west of **Clermont-Ferrand**. The marvellous Auvergne surrounds you as the circuit runs through the woods and mountains of this volcanic part of the Massif Central. Drive the twisty track and marvel at how the modern racing car can be driven at three or four times the speed you will be doing. There are scores of other attractions in the neighbourhood to fill your days with interest.

The **Le Mans** racing circuit is completely different. South of the town, between the N23 and the N138, it has long straights, sudden 90-degree turns and man-made chicanes. This historic circuit tells the story of motor sport—full of magnificent events but unhappily, some tragic ones, too. Do the whole circuit and learn, at first hand, just what the 24-hours endurance test is all about.

Not only is the **Monte-Carlo** circuit different from the other two—it is unique amongst all the world's racing tracks. It is run in the streets of Monte-Carlo itself; it starts in the Boulevard Albert 1st, climbs sharply up to the Casino, twists and turns down to the sea, then has its fastest stretch through a tunnel, back to the port at La Condamine, past the swimming pool, and finally, a 360-degree turn back to the start. It is a pulse-quickening event; if you have a chance to be there on the day, don't miss it. Drive the circuit at any time; your interest, the next time you see it on TV, will be sharper and your *know-how* increased.

Other small circuits dotted throughout France are at **Pau** (in the area of the *Gare*); at **Magny-Cours** (south of **Nevers** on the N7); at **Prenois** (north-west of **Dijon**) and at **Nogaro** (north-east of **Aire-s-l'Adour**—itself north of Pau).

There are several interesting **Motor Museums**: especially good is the one at **Compiègne** where vehicles from 2000 years ago, through to some of the first cars built, will intrigue children and adults alike.

Another one well worth bringing to your attention is the Musée de l'Automobile Henri Malatre—north of **Lyon** on the eastern banks of the Saône (use the D433). Some of the most celebrated and earliest makes of cars are amongst the 200 or so exhibits. It really is worth making a short and easy detour off the A6 Autoroute.

Near **Mulhouse**—in Alsace, is the remarkable collection of Schlumpf Bugatti cars—the Musée des Travailleurs—where hundreds of cars are all housed under one roof. Enquire locally, beforehand, to determine opening hours.

There is a fine museum with 200 exhibits at the **Le Mans** Racing Circuit.

Changing the scene once more, there are three famous **Hillclimbs** you should visit: all provide exhilarating motoring, and those who get to their summits are rewarded with breathtaking panoramas. **Mont Revard** towers over **Aix-les-Bains**; the Alps, Lac Bourget and a circle of country lie below you. The **Col de Rousset** is at the southern end of the Vercors and north of **Die**—it's the *grandfather* of hillclimbs. Finally, don't miss the climb of **Mont Ventoux**; famous, or infamous perhaps, in cycling history, but the scene of many memorable motor sport climbs too!

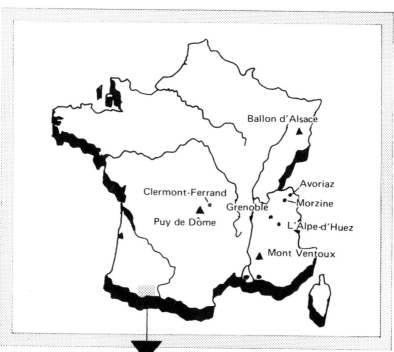

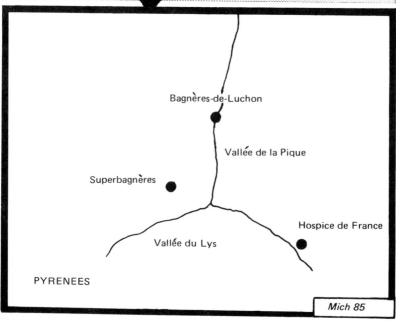

TOUR DE FRANCE HIGHLIGHTS

Each year, I follow with avid interest the progress of the Tour de France cycle race. Sports of all kinds capture my attention—but this annual body-shattering event is, for me, the epitome of bravery and endurance. The interest goes much deeper than most other sports because I know the country they cover, the risks they must take, the unbelievable depths of human energy they must draw on: how do they do it?

I am going to give you six examples of the torture the cyclists inflict upon themselves; there could be dozens more. My six *stages* could have qualified for inclusion under other headings—particularly the chapter called *Mountain-top Views*: each one of them lies in superb country and rewards any diversion you make to see it.

The first is the unique **Puy de Dôme**, west of **Clermont-Ferrand**. An old volcano, it looks like a giant cone with the Temple of Mercury, built by the Romans, on its summit. The narrow climb to the top is a *timed* stage: each man on his own—against the clock; it must be 1465 metres of sheer torture. The Puy is deeply immersed in French history; it offers exceptional views and must not be missed.

Far to the east, in the Vosges mountains, is another soul-sapping climb: up the hairpin bends of the Col du Ballon—better known as the **Ballon d'Alsace**. You, in your car, can make the trip from north to south, or vice versa: but whichever way you do it, take your time and be certain to make the short walk to the *table d'orientation* on the Ballon itself where the panorama, on clear days, can include Mont Blanc. This southern edge of the Vosges includes some of its best forests—enjoy them.

The high Alps and their numerous terrors must provide many sleepless nights for the cyclists before they set out on their three-week *tour*. Two of the worst climbs zig-zag up to villages that are better known as winter-sports resorts: **Avoriaz** and **L'Alpe-d'Huez**. Avoriaz (1800 metres) sits nearly 1000 metres above **Morzine**. As pretty as all the countryside is, that 14 kilometres climb must be a vivid reminder to the competitors that their worst fears are correct. And they know that more climbs are yet to come!

L'Alpe-d'Huez is just as bad. It is to the east of **Grenoble** and the 12 kilometres road climbs, in 22 zig-zags, over 1000 metres from the valley floor!

Mont Ventoux, sitting like a sentinel, guarding both the Rhône Valley and Provence, is another infamous climb. It was here, in 1967, that Tommy Simpson died; he was the most famous of British road cyclists. Ventoux is an extinct volcano: its hot, steep sides are frightening, even to drivers in safe cars; imagine the horror in racing cyclists' minds as they descend at speed. This *sporting* stage climbs over 1500 metres in just fifteen kilometres. I can think of no more cruel setting for any sporting event: imagine what it must be like on a blistering summer day.

The sixth example is in the **Pyrénées**—the climb from **Bagnères-de-Luchon** to **Superbagnères**; it is just as steep and just as much a killer as any of the others. Superbagnères, like Avoriaz and L'Alpe-d'Huez, is a winter-sports resort. All the countryside south of Luchon is attractive and deserves your time. You will see something of the **Vallée du Lys** during the early part of your 1200 metres climb; in the spring the southern end of the valley is worth exploring, full of cascading torrents and waterfalls. A second valley—**Vallée de la Pique**—runs south-east from Luchon to the **Hospice de France**. Many pleasures await the visitor prepared to explore this delightful corner of France: superb forests, high mountains, streams and waterfalls; the best bonus of all is that the narrow roads go nowhere. The chances are you will have all of it to yourself—make the effort to reach this south-east corner of map 85!

All these climbs are absorbing attractions for any motorist—whether they are interested in cycling or not. All of them are surrounded by attractive, inspiring country-side. Find the time to explore them on your travels in France—use your imagination to visualise just what suffering those poor cyclists have to endure.

WALKING

For the walker, France is a treasure-chest full of countless possibilities.

The keen walker will already have gained several clues from other chapters in this book to where some of the best walking country is: the Chartreuse, the Vercors, the Alps, the Pyrénées and the many *Unknown Rivers* all offer enchanting possibilities. What of specific centres which can be particularly recommended for the walker?

Brittany.

The countryside surrounding **Huelgoat** is ideal; woods, moorlands, rivers, rocks and viewpoints—all are there for the keen walker. In spring it is at its best; the tints and shades of the beech, oak, pine and spruce trees are a delight.

Normandy.

The Orne Valley is perfect walking country. Upstream from **Thury-Harcourt**, deep into the heart of *Little Switzerland*, are endless river and hill walks. I have seen it at its best in April and May—when blossom covers the fruit trees.

Massif Central.

The Auvergne hills to the south of **Royat,** and the Monts du Forez, north-east of **Ambert,** are well-known for their attractive walks. In spring, when the wild flowers carpet the pastures, it is perfect walking terrain.

Provence.

The Chaîne des Alpilles—south of **Avignon**—are a self-contained, strange outcrop of hills. Close by are many examples of Roman architecture (see *Roman France*—page 69). Avoid this hot, blistering countryside at the height of summer.

Savoie.

Endless possibilities exist in the Alps. For the naturalist the Ecrins National Park, west of **Briançon**, is world-renowned. The country lying east of **Cluses** is ideal for walkers; forests, pastures, high mountains and no through-roads.

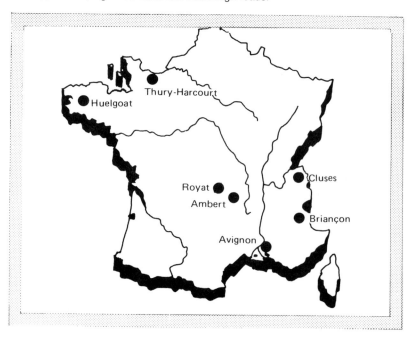

WATERWAYS

Elsewhere in this book I have written about *Ports* where outdoor enthusiasts, keen on sailing, can enjoy their sport to their hearts' content. Equally, many of the *Lakes* (page 117) have sailing facilities which provide inland sailing.

But what about those people who just want to quietly cruise the waterways of France—on canals or rivers? I describe three main areas: all of them surrounded by fine country. The special pleasures of the waterways can be enjoyed at your own pace—and there are other attractions all within easy reach.

Brittany.

The River **Vilaine** and the **Canal de Nantes–Brest** provide the best opportunities. Two centres—both near **Redon**—cater for the hire of cruisers: **Malestroit** is on the Canal, and **Arzal** is situated at the mouth of the Vilaine.

Burgundy.

The River **Yonne** and the **Canal du Nivernais** are the waterways taking you to the quieter treats of Burgundy. Many chapters describe where those are; the sailing centres of **Corbigny**, **Auxerre** and **Villeneuve-s-Yonne** are at the door of many of them.

Languedoc.

The **Canal du Midi** (from **Toulouse** to **Béziers**) and the **Canal du Rhône** (lying along the Mediterranean coast) offer, as extra bonuses, the sun and splendour of the south of France. Centres are at **Bellegarde**; at **Port Sud**, near Toulouse; and **Port Cassafières**, between Béziers and **Agde**. The waterway to the north of Toulouse takes you through green, pastoral country; the countryside is renowned for its fruit and there are many fine, *local* wines to be enjoyed. **Agen, Moissac**—with its famous abbey—and **Montauban** can all be explored. The waterways near Béziers cross quite different terrain; this is hot, dry countryside—though in most parts the canals are shaded by fine trees. Enjoy the many inexpensive *local* wines of Languedoc.

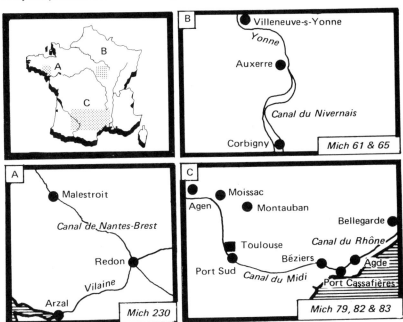

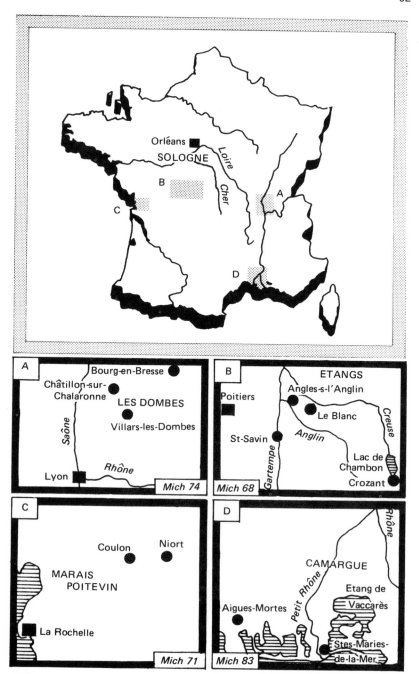

ETANGS

Etang is the French word for pond or pool. There are several areas in France where many hundreds of these sheets of water *pepper* the landscape: the *étangs* are full of wildlife and are surrounded by interesting countryside. The best example—and the first my wife and I explored—is the area lying between **Lyon** and **Bourg-en-Bresse**; it is called **Les Dombes**. For the ornithologist it is a real paradise. We can remember breaking a journey south to allow our young son, a keen bird-watcher, to quietly watch the goings-on. That stop lasted hours longer than originally planned—we were absorbed and fascinated as much as he was.

At **Villars-les-Dombes** is an excellent bird sanctuary (a small-scale Slimbridge). Nearby are one or two picturesque villages; **Châtillon-sur-Chalaronne** has changed out of all recognition over a period of 20 years—now spotless and a mass of flowers (one of many *villages fleuris* in the area). In the early spring the fields encircling the countless *étangs* are carpeted with cowslips and the hedgerows are full of the new greens of emerging buds. You can have many of the lanes to yourself—yet you are just a kilometre or two from the busiest main roads in France. So many people miss this surprising attraction of the Lyonnais country.

South of **Orléans**, between the **Loire** and the **Cher**, is another similar bit of country— the **Sologne**. It is much bigger in scale and it is different in one other respect—it is covered with thick woods. The area is renowned for its asparagus—during the season you will see the crop being harvested in the fields. You will not see the Sologne from the main roads that cross it—you will need to use the small, minor lanes and tracks. Amongst all the delightful trees—both deciduous and evergreen—are an amazing variety of birds. It is enchanting country.

Further to the south, and east of **Poitiers**, is another *Dombes*-like piece of country. It sits immediately north of the **Creuse** Valley. This is a part of France even the French choose to ignore. The Creuse, from **Le Blanc** upstream to the **Lac de Chambon**, deserves those extra hours of time needed to meander along its riverside lanes; a rewarding detour from the N20. At the southern end of the lake are the ruins of the great fortress of **Crozant**—an impressive sight and site! To the west of Le Blanc are two further river valleys you should explore. The **Anglin** is small and pretty, a tributary of the **Gartempe**. The church at **St-Savin** on the Gartempe is one of the treasures of France. Near the point the two rivers join is **Angles-s-l'Anglin**—a small village with a huge ruined castle overlooking the stream.

South-west now to the **Marais Poitevin**—north of **La Rochelle**. Not so much *étangs* here as a thousand canals and tree-lined streams (*marais* means fen). Every field is an island—where cows, goats, their milk and their feed, and all crops are moved by punt; you can make punt trips from **Coulon**, west of **Niort**. Don't bypass it: Michelin map 71 is an odd sight—but not one bit as interesting as the real thing.

The **Camargue** is, perhaps, the best known of all the regions where *étangs*, and the wildlife they spawn and protect, predominate. The **Etang de Vaccarès** has become a world-famous name. It is a Regional Nature Park in its own right, and no wonder: there is so much to interest you—flora and fauna, horses, birds of all types, water and seclusion everywhere. As if that was not enough, there is Roman Provence to the north, the ancient fortress of **Aigues-Mortes** and the old gypsy town of **Stes-Maries-de-la-Mer**. North of this town is a bird sanctuary and just west of it is the **Petit Rhône**; take a trip on the river—an ideal way to see the wildlife.

It has only been during the last few years that I have really got to know the *étangs* of France. I find them tremendously rewarding. They also offer the added bonus of taking you away from the bustling crowds and they interest child and adult alike. Don't ignore them.

94

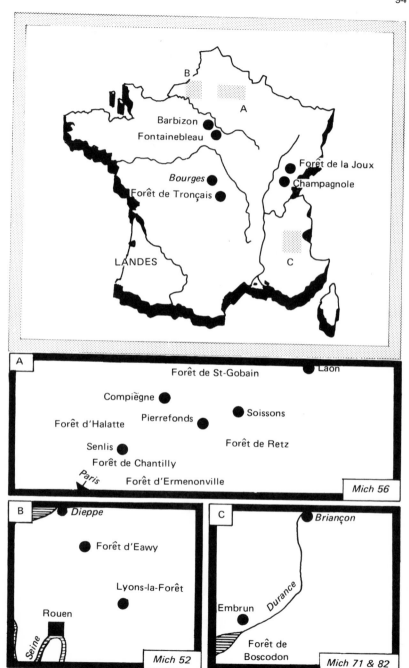

FORESTS

Life has treated me with great favour. It has been my good fortune to see the great forests and mountains of the Himalayas, and the Rockies in western North America; in addition, I have seen the superb woods on the eastern seaboard of Canada and the United States. The U.K. has tiny forests in terms of scale when compared with some of the others but they, too, are marvels of nature. France has its own special *forest* pleasures; conceived and nurtured by Mother Nature in different ways.

Perhaps one of the best is also one of the smallest, hidden in the very heart of France—the **Forêt de Tronçais**, a treasure-chest of magnificent oak trees. Its future will be as interesting as its past. Careful regeneration since the war, and thinning-out in the decades to come, will ensure by the end of the century that some handsome specimens will be growing there. This forest is best seen in summer.

Fontainebleau is at its best when it wears its glowing autumn colours. Oak, beech and Scots pine are the trees that flourish in this vast green lung of Paris. It is surrounded by so many of the roots of French history; it is easy to reach and is covered with tracks and roads which open up so many vistas. **Barbizon**, having a long association with artists, is a special attraction. The strange outcrops of rocks are another interest—much used in training rock climbers.

My favourite woods are near my home—the beech forests of the Chilterns. Each autumn, for perhaps no more than a week or two, the heart beats faster as they put on their glowing, glittering *show*; how sad that it comes just once a year!

The beech forests of France are equally breathtaking. The best are in Normandy and the greatest of all of them are the forests surrounding **Lyons-la-Forêt** (east of **Rouen**) and the **Forêt d'Eawy** (north-east of Rouen). I have seen the beech-glades in spring—carpets of bluebells stretching in all directions; the same glades, in autumn, become copper sheets that blanket the ground below the trees. Giant, proud, ancient trees; the rustling leaves whisper their secret messages to you.

North-east of Paris are several great forests: **Compiègne** is the most famous. Perhaps you will just want to lose yourself in the glades; a shame, as much history surrounds you. There is the palace at Compiègne; the forbidding castle at **Pierrefonds**; the railway coach deep in the forest where Hitler, in his revengeful way, saw the French capitulate at the start of the Second World War—that same coach had seen the signing of the 1918 Armistice.

Other forests surrounding Compiègne are the **Forêt de St-Gobain**, west of **Laon**; the Forêt de Retz, south-west of **Soissons**; the **Forêt de Chantilly**; the **Forêt d'Halatte**, to the north of **Senlis**; and finally, the **Forêt d'Ermenonville** (a special favourite of mine), south-east of Senlis. At weekends all these forests are crowded.

Far to the east is the best of all the pine forests of France—the **Forêt de la Joux**. It sits north-east of **Champagnole** and is criss-crossed by roads which make it easy to see the huge specimens—only bettered in the Rockies. One particular tree you should seek out is the *Sapin Président* with a circumference of four metres. An extra pleasure of this Jura forest are the many streams and lakes.

The forests of the Vosges mountains and the Alps are well-known to many travellers. One particular small forest known to precious few is south of **Embrun**, the **Forêt de Boscodon**. Fine mountain country encircles it—you will have it to yourself.

On the west coast is the largest of all French forests—the **Landes**. Man-made and just one century old, the pine forests were planted to save the land from becoming a vast desert. Today, for its keepers, it produces a harvest of turpentine; for the tourist, it releases that delightful perfume that only a pine forest can offer.

All the forests listed above should not be bypassed at any time during the year, but particularly in the spring and autumn when they are at their very best.

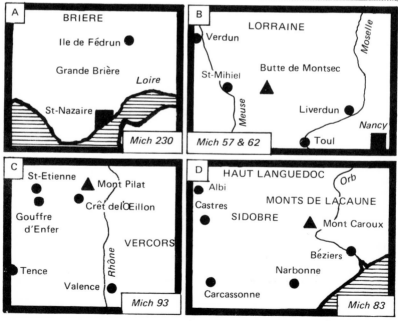

REGIONAL NATURE PARKS

Some of the happiest and most delightful of memories my wife and I have of France came as a result of making the effort to get off the beaten track to discover the incomparable treasures that Nature keeps to herself: unless you research, navigate and set aside the time needed to explore, you too, will pass them by.

There are a number of Regional Nature Parks throughout France. I am going to highlight most of them; particularly those that are easy to get to—many being within an hour or so of the great *through* routes!

Surprisingly, Brittany has one of the most unusual parks—immediately north of **St-Nazaire**—called Parc Régional de **Brière**. It is on a marshy stretch of land called the **Grande Brière**—see it in May and June when the flowers are at their best (particularly yellow irises). Take a trip on a punt through the waterways; be certain to explore the **Ile de Fédrun**, right in the heart of the marshland.

The Regional Nature Park of **Morvan**, in Burgundy, is ignored by tens of thousands of tourists, hell-bent on roaring down the autoroutes at top speed. This park is bordered by **Avallon** in the north and **Autun** to the south; it is calm, green countryside, studded with lakes, streams and woods.

The **Lorraine** Nature Park covers a great area to the north-east of the country. I particularly like the country between **Verdun** and **Toul**. It, too, is full of lakes and woods. One highlight is the panorama from the **Butte de Montsec**, east of **St-Mihiel**; another is **Liverdun** with its fine site alongside the **Moselle**.

The **Vercors** is another Nature Park—you can reach it within an hour of deserting the A1 at **Valence**. I have praised it often; it is full of dense forests, high crags, unique natural curiosities, pastures and small villages—no wonder these remote, mysterious mountains were one of the main centres of the French Resistance during the last war. It is known as *Maquis* country. *Mort pour La France* say the carved words on the simple, small monuments; no finer words can be used for any epitaph.

To the east, on the far side of the **Rhône** is **Mont Pilat**, surrounded by another Nature Park taking the name of the mountain. This country is at its best in autumn; we remember vividly a warm, cloudless Sunday we spent in the southern part of this area as we drove towards **Tence**. Every lane, every pasture, every wood and every hill was bathed in that clear, flawless, autumn light—the sort of day all of us remember, for the simple reason we just wished it would never come to an end. Two visits you must make are the drive and short walk to the **Crêt de l'Œillon**—an astonishing 360-degree panorama—and the **Gouffre d'Enfer** (east of **St-Etienne**).

Another vast park is the **Haut Languedoc** Regional Nature Park. It covers all the area between **Albi** and **Carcassonne** to the south and **Béziers** in the east; deserted country, full of rivers, lakes and old villages. The **Sidobre**, east of **Castres**, is a strange granite world of fantastic rock shapes. North of Béziers is the **Orb** Valley; the stretches near **Mont Caroux** (extensive panorama) are full of interest—gorges, caves and some enjoyable, inexpensive, local *Vins de Pays* to quench your thirst. The **Monts de Lacaune** are a special favourite—green, cool hills—and yet just kilometres from the dry and rocky hills north of **Narbonne**.

Some Regional Nature Parks are described in other chapters; those of the **Marais Poitevin** and the **Camargue** are detailed in *Etangs*. In the area of Normandy called *Little Switzerland* is the **Normandie-Maine** Park, centred on the charming spa of Bagnoles-de-l'Orne. The **Landes** Park is described in the *Forests* chapter. Others mentioned elsewhere are those of **Queyras** (*Roads that go Nowhere*), **Lubéron** (*Hidden Corners of Provence*), **Volcans d'Auvergne** (Auvergne is referred to in several chapters) and **Brotonne** (referred to in chapters on Normandy).

Wherever they may be, they all deserve to be explored and enjoyed.

98

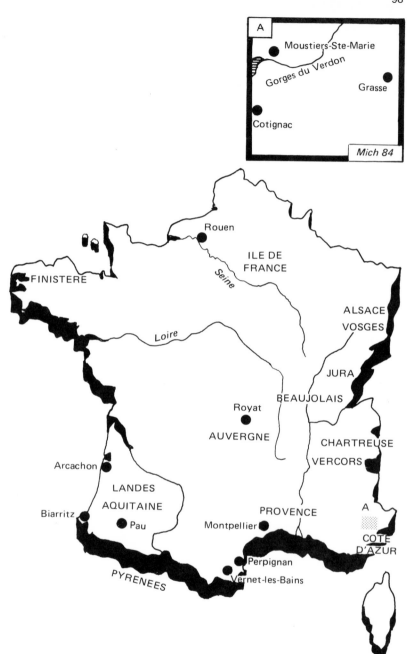

A
Moustiers-Ste-Marie
Gorges du Verdon
Grasse
Cotignac
Mich 84

Rouen
ILE DE FRANCE
Seine
FINISTERE
ALSACE
VOSGES
Loire
JURA
BEAUJOLAIS
Royat
AUVERGNE
CHARTREUSE
VERCORS
Arcachon
LANDES
AQUITAINE
Biarritz
Pau
PROVENCE
A
Montpellier
COTE D'AZUR
Perpignan
PYRENEES
Vernet-les-Bains

If you are lucky enough to be able to choose any season of the year to enjoy your holiday you are indeed fortunate: apart from missing the crowds outside the months of July and August, the time of year can be allowed to influence your decision about which region to visit. Many parts of France are lovely at any time—but are truly glorious during a few particular weeks of the year. Where are some of these spots—and when are they at their best? Here are a few ideas . . . amongst dozens.

Spring and early Summer.

All mountain country is at its best. The air is clear and sharp, the torrents are at their fullest, the first blossoms and green tints of the trees are beginning to appear and pastures are full of spring flowers; the contrast of the pure white snowfields high above combines with all these colours to make a superb rural landscape. The **Pyrénées** are one example; my wife and I have seen the countryside near **Pau** in early April, fruit blossom everywhere and thick snow still on the distant peaks—July and August cannot emulate that.

Aquitaine is at its best in April and May. We have seen primroses, daffodils, tulips, bluebells, lilacs and roses—all flowering together. The new tints on the awakening trees seem to permutate every shade of yellow, green and brown; from limes and emerald to sand and coffee.

The hills near **Moustiers-Ste-Marie** are a delight. A Romanesque church, a chapel originally built by Charlemagne (since rebuilt) and the incomparable **Gorges du Verdon**—all these are at hand. The hills between **Cotignac** and **Grasse** are enticingly lovely in early summer; carpets of colour cover terraces, walls and fields.

Where else can you enjoy the awakening best of spring? **Finistère**, Normandy and Brittany are a mass of apple blossom; in the west brilliant gorse competes to fill your eyes with colour. The **Chartreuse** and the **Vercors** (especially the river gorges in each *massif*) are a splash of new greens and ice-cold, roaring streams. The **Vosges**, the **Jura** and the **Auvergne** are all gorgeous. We have marvelled at the countless varieties of wild flowers in the green pastures of the hills south of **Royat**. These volcanic hills are all part of the Volcans d'Auvergne—a Regional Nature Park full of other pleasures to fill many hours.

I recall, too, the perfume of the lilacs alongside the River Lot . . . spring is perfection!

Autumn.

The glorious beech forests north of the **Seine** (near **Rouen**) and those of the **Ile de France** are amongst our most vivid memories; so are the Walt Disney colour-scapes of the **Chartreuse** and **Vercors**. Is there a more incomparable month than October?

Any of the wine villages and wine country are at their best when the grapes are being harvested for the new vintage. **Alsace** and the **Jura** both produce their own delectable light wines; the pastures in the Jura are full of the lilac-coloured autumn crocuses. **Beaujolais** country and the **Loire** have their own extra scenic attractions that compete with the eye-catching rows of orange and yellow vines: the Loire has its châteaux; Beaujolais its hills, woods and treasures—like nearby Cluny, Pérouges, Charlieu and dozens more.

Winter.

The Ile de France is well worth visiting. Winter allows you to see views and scenes with a new perspective; the trees and hedges are like bare bones—leafless—and you see, for the first time, sights not seen in high summer.

The **Côte d'Azur** is well known for its mild winter days; but equally so is the countryside of **Provence** and from **Montpellier** to **Perpignan** (and the sheltered spas inland like **Vernet-les-Bains**). The Southwest too is ideal: **Biarritz**; the forests of the **Landes**; **Arcachon**; usually all are amazingly mild in winter.

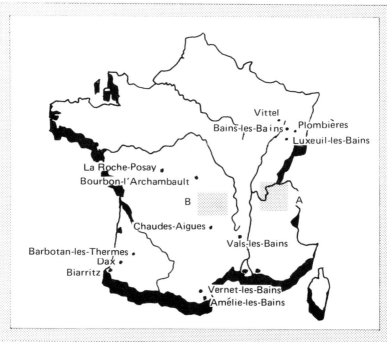

Vittel
Bains-les-Bains
Plombières
Luxeuil-les-Bains
La Roche-Posay
Bourbon-l'Archambault
B
A
Chaudes-Aigues
Barbotan-les-Thermes
Dax
Biarritz
Vals-les-Bains
Vernet-les-Bains
Amélie-les-Bains

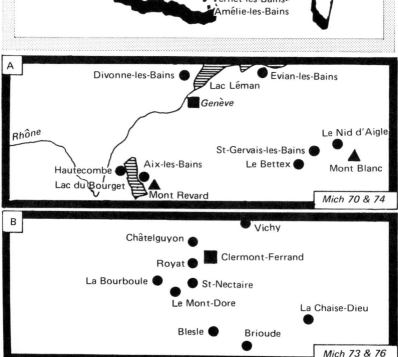

A
Divonne-les-Bains
Evian-les-Bains
Lac Léman
Genève
Rhône
Le Nid d'Aigle
St-Gervais-les-Bains
Le Bettex
Hautecombe
Aix-les-Bains
Lac du Bourget
Mont Revard
Mont Blanc
Mich 70 & 74

B
Vichy
Châtelguyon
Royat
Clermont-Ferrand
La Bourboule
St-Nectaire
Le Mont-Dore
La Chaise-Dieu
Blesle
Brioude
Mich 73 & 76

SPAS

Throughout the centuries, *taking the waters* has been a custom known to our fore-fathers; indeed, many of the famous medicinal springs in France were enthusiastically used—and their praises sung—by the Romans, 2000 years ago.

An ever increasing number of people over the years have discovered the therapeutic qualities of the springs: but whether you are taking the waters or not, all the spas listed here are worth visiting. Cures are no doubt helped by the many scenic attractions close at hand and by the clear air, the lack of noise and the parks, gardens and pools in each of the spas.

The first four are set amidst, or adjacent to, the splendid Alps.

St-Gervais-les-Bains is under the shadow of massive **Mont Blanc**; above the town, in the hills that lie to the east, is **Le Bettex**. Go there on a clear day (try the afternoon) and enjoy one of the greatest of all Alpine views. Take the tramway up to **Le Nid d'Aigle**—spectacular views all the way.

Aix-les-Bains lies on the eastern bank of the **Lac du Bourget**: Lamartine wrote his famous poem about Elvire here. On the western bank is the Abbey of **Hautecombe**, a Cistercian abbey, founded by Saint Bernard in 1125; and above the Aix is **Mont Revard** with its magnificent panoramic views of the Alps.

Evian-les-Bains is a lovely lakeside town, but the countless lanes in the hills above Evian are, for me, the special appeal of this corner of France. All this countryside is at its best in the spring or the golden autumn.

Divonne-les-Bains has a backdrop of the Jura hills—not high, but covered in a green carpet of dark woods and emerald pastures. You could lose yourself for hours in the gorges and forests of the Jura. At Divonne's doorstep is **Lac Léman** and the many boating possibilities and trips offered by that corner of Switzerland.

The Massif Central contains many spa towns—several are grouped around **Clermont-Ferrand**: **Vichy, Royat, La Bourboule, Le Mont-Dore, Châtelguyon** and **St-Nectaire**. All of them allow you to explore Auvergne; full of old volcanoes, now blanketed, like the Jura, with green pastures and forests. Auvergne is full of Roman-esque churches; those at **Blesle, St-Nectaire** (the finest of them all—it has become a legend throughout the world), and at **Brioude** are highlights. Don't miss the splendid Abbey of **La Chaise-Dieu** with its cloisters and tapestries.

Further south in the Massif Central are **Chaudes-Aigues** (it gets its hot water free from natural springs); and in the Ardèche countryside, **Vals-les-Bains**—this spa sits astride the Volane, at its junction with the River Ardèche.

In the far south, at either end of the Pyrénées, are four attractive spots: **Vernet-les-Bains** and **Amélie-les-Bains** are in sheltered valleys; both have dry, sunny climates and mountains surrounding them, and both are close to the Mediterranean.

At the Atlantic end, and north of the Pyrénées, are **Dax** (a biggish place), full of fountains bubbling forth hot spring water, and **Barbotan-les-Thermes**, a tiny place on the edge of the *département* of Gers. Both are within striking distance of the huge, sandy beaches of the coast running north from **Biarritz**; both are on the edge of the vast, man-made pine forests of the Landes. Barbotan allows you to navigate the quiet, green woods in the hills and valleys of Gers that lie to the east.

In the heart of France are **La Roche-Posay** and **Bourbon-l'Archambault**; all the secret treasures of Poitou and Berry-Bourbonnais are on hand. None of it is tourist country but all of it is pastoral perfection, with deep historical and cultural roots.

Finally, in the far north-east of France is world-famous **Vittel** which, like Vichy, is a household name. To the south-east of Vittel are small **Bains-les-Bains, Luxeuil-les-Bains** and **Plombières**. All these are super places and they offer the chance to explore the wooded Vosges mountains to the east.

102

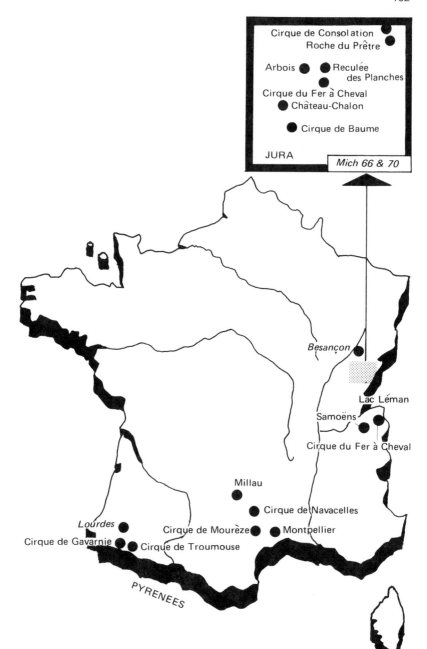

CIRQUES

One definition of *cirque* is *circus*; but that is not its meaning when applied to the country-side. The second use of the word means an *amphitheatre* of mountains.

France is richly endowed with *cirques*; inspiring sights they are too, from small-scale ones to giant examples which fill the sky with rock faces climbing high above you. Some can only be seen from the valley below—unless, that is, you are a skilled mountain climber; others can be seen from both the valley floor and from the tops of the high cliffs lining their steep sides.

The most famous—and the one that allows me to describe them at their best—is in the western Pyrénées, on the border with Spain; the **Cirque de Gavarnie**. Vertical rock faces—rising in several stages, and each stage as much as 500 metres high—surround you on three sides. The floor of the valley is a mass of rocks—like the remains of a giant battlefield. In the spring, when the melting snows pour forth their watery torrents, a dozen or more waterfalls and cascades are at their best. Nature provides many great sights on the face of the earth and this is surely one of them. It is well off the beaten track—but do see it.

Just a few kilometres away to the east is a second formidable wall of mountains—the **Cirque de Troumouse**. Not as famous as its big brother, the Gavarnie, but never-theless, it is another awe-inspiring sight, well worth seeing.

Hundreds of kilometres away—near the borders of Switzerland this time—are much smaller versions of Gavarnie. They are not so savage; their edges and sides are lined by the lovely green forests of the Jura—as a consequence they are easier on the eye and perhaps more quietly pleasing.

Seek out several of these smaller *cirques* in the **Jura**: south-west of **Arbois** is the **Cirque du Fer à Cheval** and the **Reculée des Planches**; south-east of **Château-Chalon** (this village and the town of Arbois make fine wines) is the **Cirque de Baume**. All these natural sights can be explored from the valley floor, but see them also from the roads that take you to the top of the rocky escarpments. Enjoy both alternative scenic aspects. If you can, visit the Cirque du Fer à Cheval in the spring when the River Cuisance is at its most thrilling—man cannot emulate the cascades awaiting the onlooker there.

Elsewhere in the Jura lies another *cirque* that is worth making the effort to see. The **Cirque de Consolation** is one of my favourite corners in eastern France. View it first from the **Roche du Prêtre**, high above the valley—then drive down to the lovely woods and pastures lining the many streams that come together to form the River Dessoubre. It is a glorious spot.

The Savoie mountains on the southern side of **Lac Léman** (Lake Geneva) have their own **Cirque du Fer à Cheval**—east of **Samoëns**. This is quite different from the Jura *cirques* as it is surrounded by high mountains. A vivid impression remains in my memory of when I first saw it, late in the spring—literally dozens of cascades were shooting forth the melted snows from Alpine glaciers and snowfields.

The strangest of all the French *cirques* is the hardest one to pin down on a map, and consequently the hardest to find: the **Cirque de Navacelles**. South-east of **Millau**, it is encircled by a whole series of gorges, grottoes and caves. The River Vis meanders through the *causses* (plateaux) of Larzac and Blandas, and at Navacelles forms one of the most extraordinary sights in all France—a *cirque* surrounding the loops of the river far below. West of **Montpellier** is the unusual **Cirque de Mourèze**—where a vast number of rocks, of the strangest shapes, litter the ground.

All the examples described above require a determined resolve on your part to put aside the time to seek them out; they are well away from the tourist traps, like all the *hidden*, natural sights of France.

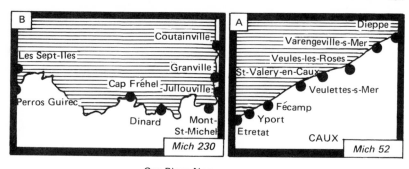

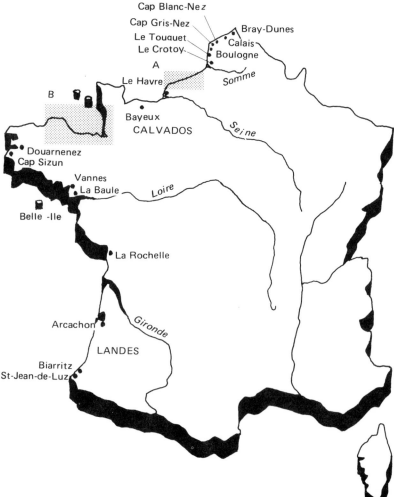

The varied coastlines of France are a dramatic example of how much the country differs from north to south and east to west. Her 3000 kilometres of varied seaboard is a living testament of how much she has been favoured by Mother Nature: whatever her visitors' tastes may be for coastal scenery, they will find, somewhere in France, what they are looking for. Bear in mind that in July and August it is well nigh impossible to avoid the crowds of holidaymakers.

I cannot pretend to have exhausted all the possibilities on this page. (Remember: the beaches of France are described in another chapter.) Here are some of my favourite sections of the very long Atlantic coastline.

The North Sea coast is a line of sand from the Belgian border at **Bray-Dunes** to **Calais**. Beyond Calais the coastline turns 90 degrees due south: the white chalk cliffs of this corner have two famous *Caps* as sentries—the massive **Cap Gris-Nez** and **Cap Blanc-Nez**. They rival the white cliffs of Dover—on clear days the latter are visible far across the English Channel to the north. Will the cliffs of France and England be joined one day by a tunnel or a bridge?

Beyond **Boulogne** are kilometres of rolling sand dunes; past **Le Touquet** right down to **Le Crotoy**. My family and I have walked those deserted dunes in mid winter; invigorating and windy hours, but, nevertheless, healthy and enjoyable ones.

Beyond the **Somme** is the lovely coastline of the **Caux** region of Normandy. There are magnificent white cliffs stretching from **Dieppe** to **Etretat** and, studded like jewels along their length, are many villages and small ports. Make the effort, if you use the ports of **Le Havre** and Dieppe, to search them out, rather than blasting away from them. Their names? **Varengeville-s-Mer**, **Veules-les-Roses**, **St-Valery-en-Caux**, **Veulettes-s-Mer**, **Fécamp**, **Yport** and Etretat. For the best views use all the narrow lanes that link these places together.

Beyond the **Seine** is the **Calvados** coast, from the sophisticated resorts at its eastern end to the D-Day beaches north of **Bayeux**. The west-facing shoreline of the Cotentin Peninsula is more like Brittany, full of sandy beaches and small resorts: **Coutainville**, **Granville** and **Jullouville** are three of them. West of **Mont-St-Michel** is the *Emerald* Coast dotted with delightful, tiny resorts and studded with numerous protected beaches; all of it is ideal for family holidays.

The considerable length of the northern Brittany coastline, plus the southern coast stretching down to **La Baule**, could easily fill every day of a very long holiday with endless pleasures; it is a treasure-trove of fishing villages, coves, sandy beaches and rocky headlands, which take the brunt of the Atlantic waves hammering against them. Some of the special pleasures of this lengthy stretch are covered elsewhere in this book. For the ornithologist, it is a true paradise: **Cap Fréhel**, west of **Dinard**; **Les Sept-Iles**, near **Perros Guirec**; **Cap Sizun** near **Douarnenez**; and **Belle-Ile**, off Vannes, are all bird reserves open to the public.

South of the **Loire** are great stretches of sandy beaches—ideal for children. The coastline here has many added bonuses for children and adults alike—islands, new resorts and old ports like **La Rochelle**.

The Bay of Biscay seaboard comes to an end in a strange way. Nature has drawn a straight line due south from the mouth of the **Gironde**; it is a 200 kilometres long beach, backed by the vast, man-made forests of the **Landes**. **Arcachon** is a fine resort beside its calm inland bay, full of wildlife and oyster beds. The Atlantic coastline comes to an end at the world-renowned resorts of **Biarritz** and **St-Jean-de-Luz**. Make certain you see—and hear—the Atlantic rollers crashing in against these long beaches of the Landes; a memorable sight, particularly when the winds are at their strongest and blowing from the south-west.

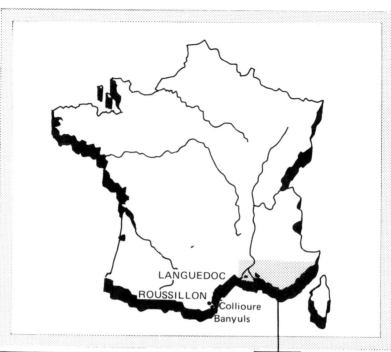

LANGUEDOC

ROUSSILLON

Collioure
Banyuls

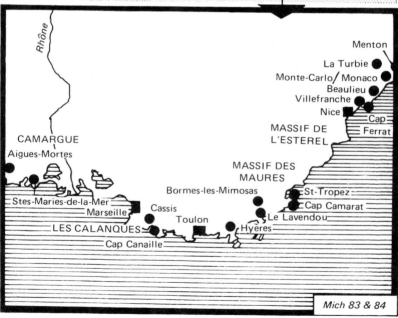

Rhône

Menton
La Turbie
Monte-Carlo / Monaco
Beaulieu
Villefranche
Nice
Cap
Ferrat

MASSIF DE
L'ESTEREL

CAMARGUE
Aigues-Mortes

MASSIF DES
MAURES

Bormes-les-Mimosas

St-Tropez
Cap Camarat

Stes-Maries-de-la-Mer
Marseille

Cassis

Toulon

Le Lavendou

LES CALANQUES

Hyères

Cap Canaille

Mich 83 & 84

The Mediterranean coast of France starts at its southern end with the Spanish border and ends hundreds of kilometres to the north-east at the frontier with Italy. High mountains come tumbling down to the sea: the Pyrénées run west to east and, at the point where they meet the Mediterranean, there are several small fishing ports—**Collioure** and **Banyuls** amongst them—unknown to most travellers in France; the Alps stretch north from the three famous Riviera Corniches linking **Menton** and **Nice**—household names throughout the world. Simplicity and sophistication can be found at the two ends of this remarkable coastline.

The Pyrénées end has another difference too: fine, strong red and sweet, golden wines come from the **Roussillon** area surrounding the villages just mentioned.

As the concave coast makes its great sweep north and then east to **Marseille**, it passes through the **Languedoc**: this is a *new* coastline with many resorts constructed since the war. Scenically, it is all wretchedly dull, but, if sun and sand is what you want, this is where you should head for.

At the mouth of the **Rhône** is perhaps the strangest part of the coastline—the **Camargue**. Who amongst you have made the detour to the old fortified port of **Aigues-Mortes**—inland now, deserted by the receding sea—and **Stes-Maries-de-la-Mer**? Legend has it that the first Christians landed here: Mary of Bethany; Mary Magdalene; Mary, mother of James; Lazarus and Sarah. It is here the gypsies come, once each year on May 24/25, to pay homage to Sarah, their patron Saint.

Beyond Marseille is the most exciting, the wildest and the most inaccessible bit of Mediterranean coast—known as **Les Calanques**. Cliffs, hundreds of metres high, drop vertically into the blue sea. They are etched with long and deep coves—*calanques*; these strange, completely silent sights can only be visited by boat—from **Cassis**. Once more my advice is simple—don't miss them.

Immediately beyond Cassis are the towering white limestone cliffs of **Cap Canaille** —over 300 metres high; the superb views they provide do not require exertion on your part as your car will take you to the cliff-tops.

Beyond **Toulon** is the **Massif des Maures**. The coast road from **Hyères** to **St-Tropez** is one of the best in France; those motorists who persist in using the shortest possible route to the Côte d'Azur are depriving themselves of a marvellous drive.

Hyères was once the home of R. L. Stevenson: he called it the 'loveliest spot in the Universe.' **Bormes-les-Mimosas** does justice to its name: it is quiet and sits inland above the coast. From **Le Lavandou** eastwards are a series of beaches, all with the same backdrop of the dark, wooded hills of the Maures. Don't make the mistake of using the main road north into St-Tropez; the alternative D93 is far more rewarding—especially if you make the short deviation to **Cap Camarat.**

From St-Tropez to **Nice** the coastline passes through villages and towns—household names throughout the world. Drive along the coast road to the south of the **Massif de l'Esterel** in the twilight; it is especially interesting at that hour as the setting sun accentuates the reds of the dark, craggy mountains to the north.

The coastline ends with the spectacular Riviera Corniches. There are no less than three alternative roads from **Nice** to **Menton**. Drive them all—they are full of scenic pleasures with sea-scapes and mountain views at every bend in the road. Amazingly, even a new autoroute has been built high above the sea.

There are several attractions you must not miss. Amongst them are: **La Turbie** with its *Trophée des Alpes;* **Villefranche** with its busy harbours (thankfully isolated from the N98 road); attractive **Beaulieu**; **Cap Ferrat**, the most famous piece of real estate anywhere in the world; and finally, **Monte-Carlo** and **Monaco**—with palaces, museums, parks and a world-famous harbour.

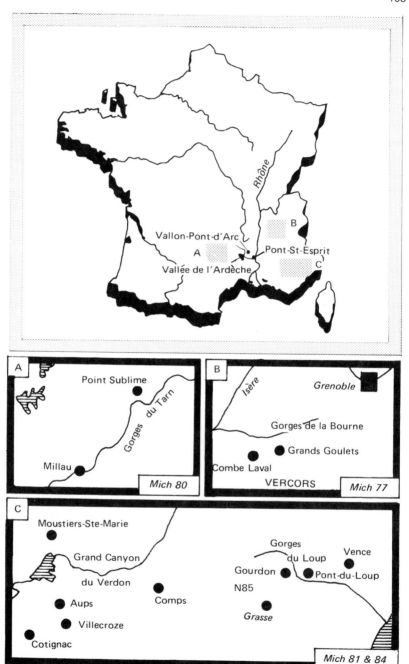

A

Point Sublime

Gorges du Tarn

Millau

Mich 80

B

Isère

Grenoble

Gorges de la Bourne

Grands Goulets

Combe Laval

VERCORS

Mich 77

C

Moustiers-Ste-Marie

Grand Canyon

du Verdon

Aups

Comps

Villecroze

Cotignac

Gorges du Loup

Vence

Gourdon

Pont-du-Loup

N85

Grasse

Mich 81 & 84

GORGES—THE FAMOUS ONES

Amongst European countries, France stands alone in its vast variety of spectacular canyons, gorges and river valleys. They are spread throughout the mountains of the country: some are known throughout the world and it is these that are listed here. Amongst the lesser-known ones are half a dozen or so worth bringing to your attention: seek them out as they will not fail to please—see the following chapter.

The most breathtaking and impressive of them all is the **Grand Canyon du Verdon**. It is a small-scale Grand Canyon of Colorado; small-scale or not, in Europe it has no rival. It is a 20 kilometres long, deep scar in the limestone plateau—at places the floor is over 700 metres below the viewpoints lining its edges.

The Corniche Sublime runs along the southern line of the canyon's edge: drive it slowly, stop often at the special parking spots, and then walk to the best viewpoints. Don't miss the northern, newer road—the Route des Crêtes. Most tourists ignore it; set a day aside to see everything the whole area keeps to itself. **Moustiers-Ste-Marie**, the start of the drive, is a favourite Provençal village of mine. All the countryside surrounding the Grand Canyon du Verdon deserves your time and attention. The few tourists that come this way tend to stick like magnets to the **N85**; what a pity as the many Provençal villages are worth exploring. Amongst them are **Aups**, **Comps**, **Cotignac**, and **Villecroze** (fine caves); they are at their best in May and June.

Due west from the Verdon, on the other side of the **Rhône**, is the **Vallée de l'Ardèche**—from **Vallon-Pont-d'Arc**, south-east, to **Pont-St-Esprit**, where the River Ardèche joins the **Rhône**. On the northern side of the river, high above the rushing rapids, is a new, thrilling road—one of the most amazing and rewarding drives in France. It is at its best in early spring, when the river, unharnessed as it is, is in flood. Once more you should set aside plenty of time to do justice to one of Nature's great treasures: stop at Pont-d'Arc, a natural stone arch, and at the many viewpoints on the road.

At the southern end of the Massif Central are the **Gorges du Tarn**. They are equally breathtaking when viewed from the roads on the cliff edges (especially from the **Point Sublime**) or when the riverside roads in the valley are followed. Spend a day enjoying the endless distractions, but, even that may not satisfy you, as more happy hours can be spent in a punt on the quieter stretches or, alternatively, you may want to go back one evening and see some of the illuminated sections. Ensure you make diversions to the country lying to the north and south of the Tarn. The *causses* (plateaux) hide many astonishing sights below their surfaces—see the chapter *Grottoes & Caves*. To the north-west of **Millau** are two man-made lakes, each of which provides an opportunity for water-based sports.

A favourite area of mine, the **Vercors**, hides within its mountainous heart some of its own special attractions. The spring and autumn colours of the trees are both equally pleasing, though spring is perhaps the best time to use the roads in the **Gorges de la Bourne**, the **Grands Goulets** and the **Combe Laval**. They are three quite different natural attractions but each one of the three will surprise and thrill you. The roads are narrow and need careful driving but if you take it quietly and slowly your efforts will be rewarded richly indeed. Vast forests, craggy mountains and green pastures all combine in an inspiring, quiet way.

Finally the **Gorges du Loup**—seen by more tourists than any of the others, simply because it sits within a few kilometres of the towns on the Côte d'Azur. It is not as magnificent as the others but, nevertheless, it is a great natural sight of the region. Drive the route starting from **Vence** and descending into **Pont-du-Loup**. Continue north up the valley and return south again, climbing up to **Gourdon**. Just before reaching Gourdon enjoy the impressive views of the mass of mountains across the Gorges du Loup and the river far below on its way to the Mediterranean.

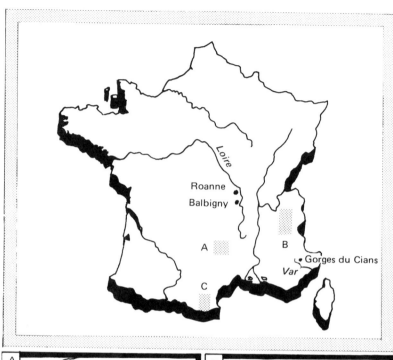

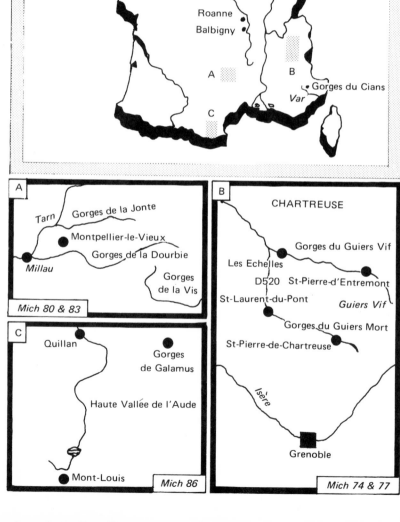

A

Tarn

Gorges de la Jonte

Montpellier-le-Vieux

Gorges de la Dourbie

Millau

Gorges
de la Vis

Mich 80 & 83

C

Quillan

Gorges
de Galamus

Haute Vallée de l'Aude

Mont-Louis

Mich 86

B

CHARTREUSE

Gorges du Guiers Vif

Les Echelles

D520   St-Pierre-d'Entremont

St-Laurent-du-Pont   *Guiers Vif*

Gorges du Guiers Mort

St-Pierre-de-Chartreuse

Isère

Grenoble

Mich 74 & 77

GORGES—THE UNKNOWN ONES

The following are amongst the less well-known gorges, found somewhat off the beaten track: few tourists will have seen them, for the simple reason that—assuming they had heard of them in the first place—they will not have made the simple navigation effort required to seek them out. Don't make the same mistake.

The River **Loire** provides the best example of what I mean. From **Roanne**, it makes a huge swing, first north, and then west, towards the Atlantic: but south of Roanne—to its source—it is quite a different river; a mountain stream passing through many narrow, torrent-like sections. One such section is just south of Roanne, unknown to most people. Use the lanes that run along the banks of the river between Roanne and **Balbigny**. You will get a pleasant surprise indeed in this lovely bit of country; it will certainly take an hour or more of your time than the alternative of using the N82—but that is a tiny price to pay for such pleasures.

North of **Grenoble** is one of my favourite parts of France—the entrancing, secretive mountains of the **Chartreuse** Massif. Within its high walls it hides many secrets from the majority of tourists, hell-bent on their blinkered motorway speeding. Amongst those secrets are two gorges: the **Gorges du Guiers Vif**—between **St-Pierre-d'Entremont** and **Les Echelles**—and further south, the **Gorges du Guiers Mort**—between **St-Laurent-du-Pont** and **St-Pierre-de-Chartreuse**.

Explore both of them. Start with the River **Guiers Vif** at its source—six kilometres south-east of St-Pierre-d'Entremont. Drive its entire length to the main road—the **D520**; then climb the Guiers Mort Valley up to St-Pierre-de-Chartreuse. Both are narrow, boulder-strewn and surrounded by cool, dark woods and verdant countryside; they are at much their best in early spring when the new greens add brightness and light to the pure water of the crashing cascades—the rivers are in full flood during April and May. Spend as much time as you can exploring the forests and pastures of the Massif; use the deserted mountain roads and forest tracks. I guarantee you happy, inspiring hours—you will return often in the years to come.

Far to the south, just before the Alps fall sharply into the Mediterranean, are the **Gorges du Cians**. Steep cliffs, coming so close together that they nearly touch, overhang the narrow road; dark red rocks add extra splendour to the rushing torrent as it falls steeply down to the River **Var**. It is quite different from the Verdon but just as thrilling—you feel part of this extrovert *show* put on by Mother Nature. The road is narrow and you must take great care.

Near neighbours of the **Tarn**, but rarely visited, are the **Gorges de la Jonte**, the **Gorges de la Dourbie** (detour to the strange rock formations at **Montpellier-le Vieux**) and the **Gorges de la Vis**. You will need to stop continually to admire the views and take lots of spare film to capture all the spectacular sights.

Further south are two final examples you must seek out.

The **Haute Vallée de l'Aude**, from its source near **Mont-Louis** downstream to **Quillan**, is full of scenic attractions: high mountains, some glorious forests and spectacular gorges all unite to put on an impressive *show*. I spent a lovely April day soaking up the pleasures of this enchanting valley. The clear, blue sky helped, of course. But it was the remarkable way that colours and sounds combined to captivate my senses that, even today, leaves a clear picture in my head. There were the many shades and tints of the trees in the forests rising steeply above the roaring river—in flood as the snows melted and fed it with clear, pure water; on the mountain tops were huge splashes of snow, and above it all a turquoise sky.

Before you leave the area: to the east of Quillan are the **Gorges de Galamus**. Make the short diversion to this minor attraction; it is quite different from the Aude—and is well worth seeing.

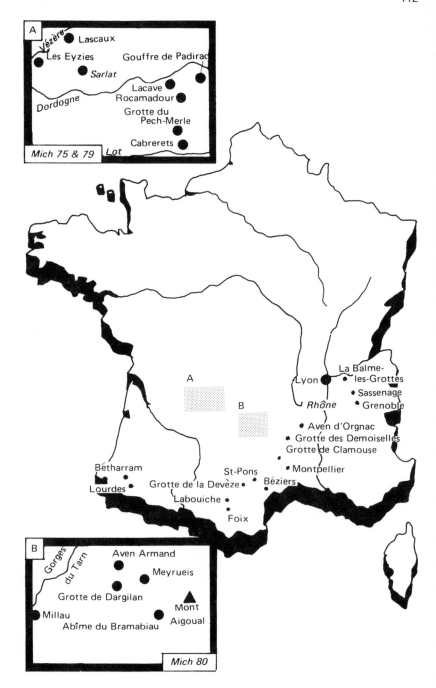

A

Vézère — Lascaux

Les Eyzies

Gouffre de Padirac

Sarlat

Dordogne

Lacave
Rocamadour

Grotte du
Pech-Merle

Cabrerets

Lot

Mich 75 & 79

A

B

Lyon

La Balme-
les-Grottes

Sassenage

Rhône

Grenoble

Aven d'Orgnac

Grotte des Demoiselles

Grotte de Clamouse

Bétharram

St-Pons

Montpellier

Lourdes

Grotte de la Devèze

Béziers

Labouiche

Foix

B

Gorges
du Tarn

Aven Armand

Meyrueis

Grotte de Dargilan

Mont
Aigoual

Millau

Abîme du Bramabiau

Mich 80

It would take a lifetime to see all the *surface* attractions of France. But, amazingly, France has more than its fair share of *underground sights*; a wealth of caves, caverns and grottoes—spread across the length and breadth of the country.

They fall into three types: the caves of prehistoric men, some decorated by our unknown forefathers; the massive underground caverns, some as large as modern halls and studded with bizarre stalagmites and stalactites; and finally, the grottoes which, whilst not calling for the skills of pot-holers, will, nevertheless, require a fair bit of effort if they are to be explored by the average visitor.

The best of all the prehistoric caves are in the Dordogne region; at **Lascaux** and **Les Eyzies**. The Lascaux cave, unhappily, has been closed to ordinary tourists for some years; it was discovered as recently as 1940, but its opening to the world at large has been harmful to the amazing paintings of horses, deer and bison.

Further down the **Vézère** Valley, at Les Eyzies, are several caves where you can view paintings and carvings from prehistoric times: Abri du Cap Blanc, Font-de-Gaume and the Grotte des Combarelles (all three to the east of Les Eyzies). There are at least half a dozen more minor caves in the vicinity of this lovely town.

Further south, near **Cabrerets**, and just north of the **Lot** Valley, is the **Grotte du Pech-Merle**. This famous place, apart from its wall paintings and carvings has, as a bonus, some outstanding natural stone formations; fine stalagmites and shapes like saucers, plates and wheels fill the caves with unusual interest.

Of the various caverns to be seen, the best of the lot is the **Gouffre de Padirac**, where, hundreds of metres underground, you can travel for several kilometres on a punt on the dark River Styx. It is a fantastic world of stalagmites, stalactites, lakes and rivers —it is one of the most rewarding visits you can make in France.

Back at **Les Eyzies** is the Grotte du Grand Roc—a much simpler affair, with no water or long underground descents but, nevertheless, it rewards all visitors with a marvellous display of natural rock carvings.

Further east, near the **Gorges du Tarn**, is the breathtaking **Aven Armand**. Its spectacular, floodlit underground hall is truly a petrified *forest*—the Forêt Vierge. Further east still, south of the River Ardèche, is the **Aven d'Orgnac** (*Aven* has the same meaning as our Celtic *Avon*—a river arising from a natural spring); colossal stalagmites and mighty halls make this cave an impressive sight.

The **Grotte des Demoiselles** is another of the great *dry* caverns. Magnificent stone formations have been shaped by Nature over the centuries; you'll find particularly fine stalactites and stalagmites in cathedral-sized caverns.

Of the grottoes where water plays a significant part in adding to their interest, those at **Bétharram** (just west of **Lourdes**) and at **La Balme-les-Grottes** (near the **Rhône** and east of **Lyon**) are particularly absorbing. A third, similar grotto, is the subterranean river at **Labouiche**, near **Foix**, in the eastern Pyrénées.

There are many other grottoes and caves—wet and dry—throughout France. Some of these are listed here in note form with a brief indication of their location and the nearest town of any size.

Amongst the *wet* caves are:

Abîme du Bramabiau—east of **Millau**, near **Mont Aigoual**;
Sassenage, near **Grenoble**—an *erosion* cavern.

Amongst the *dry* caves are:

Grotte de Dargilan, east of **Millau**, just before reaching **Meyrueis**;
Lacave, just north of **Rocamadour** and alongside the **Dordogne**;
Grotte de la Devèze, near **St-Pons**, west of **Béziers**;
Grotte de Clamouse, west of **Montpellier**.

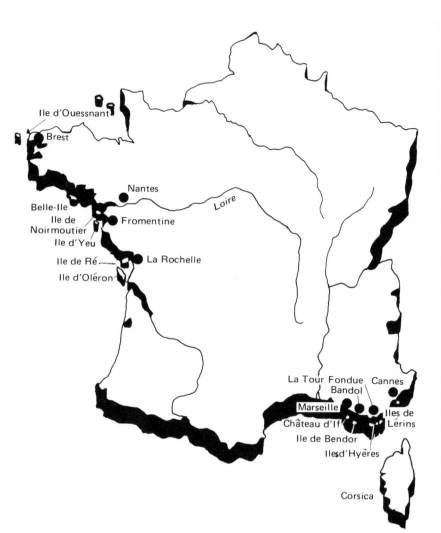

Ile d'Ouessant

Brest

Nantes

Belle-Ile
Ile de
Noirmoutier
Ile d'Yeu

Fromentine

Loire

Ile de Ré

La Rochelle

Ile d'Oléron

La Tour Fondue
Bandol

Cannes

Marseille

Iles de
Lérins

Château d'If

Ile de Bendor

Iles d'Hyères

Corsica

ISLANDS

France suffers particularly badly when its islands are compared with those lying off the coast of the United Kingdom (are there any islands to match the majestic ones adjacent to the Western Highlands?). One exception, of course, is **Corsica**: it could justify its own mini-version of this book. It has thrilling mountain country with some of the best motoring enjoyment to be found anywhere (are there any roads without bends in Corsica?); deserted roads which in turn take you to spectacular viewpoints, to pretty valleys and gorges, and lead you to the isolated small ports and villages on the western side of the island.

After Corsica there remain just a handful of possible alternatives that are worth highlighting: two are off the coast of Brittany; four are situated in the Bay of Biscay between **Nantes** and **La Rochelle**; and several tiny islands—tiny compared with Corsica—bask in the Mediterranean.

In making the sea trip from **Brest** to **Ile d'Ouessant** (Ushant), there is no more dramatic and effective way of grasping why this north-west corner of Brittany's coast is so dangerous. In the summer months it is at its quiet best; in the worst of the winter, it is a thundering, dangerous and cruel sea. The island itself is just seven kilometres long and its northern coastline is famous for its rocky shores. It is part of the Armorique Regional Nature Park; the sea birds that nest there are the highlight for any naturalist making the trip.

To the south-east, much further down the Brittany coastline, is **Belle-Ile**; there is no better place in France if you want real peace and quiet. A variety of differing scenes will intrigue you: rocky cliffs; small valleys; fine trees; a sheltered east coast and its most famous sight—the Apothicairerie Grotto. Its name comes from the cormorants' nests that line the rocky cliffs—unusual, too, is the blue-green colour of the sea in the narrow inlet.

South of the **Loire** are two smallish islands. **Ile de Noirmoutier** is reached by a toll bridge—it has sandy beaches and woods, but little else. **Fromentine** is at the point the bridge leaves the mainland—it also serves as the departure port for a second island called **Ile d'Yeu**. The southern coast of this island is famous for its rocky headlands— called the Côte Sauvage. It has much else to appreciate—small ports, sandy beaches and a general air of picturesque charm.

Further down the French coast are two more islands—both bigger than Belle-Ile. The southernmost of the two is **Ile d'Oléron**, France's second largest island. Both are famous for their luminous light, their sunsets, their oysters, their shrimps, their sands and sea air. Oléron is a favourite of mine—reached by the longest *pont-viaduc* in France, over three kilometres long. Make a special effort to visit this island. Off **La Rochelle** is the **Ile de Ré**, smaller and not as interesting.

In the Mediterranean are four islands worth a *deviation*.

The **Château d'If**, near **Marseille**, is famous for its legendary Count of Monte Cristo—from Dumas' classic story; it has always made an effective prison.

The **Ile de Bendor**, off **Bandol**, is a tiny island—developed by Monsieur Ricard of *apéritif* fame; a Provençal village, museum and zoo make it an interesting port of call for visitors to Bandol and Sanary.

Further east are the **Iles d'Hyères**—also called the *golden isles*. The Ile de Porquerolles, quickly and easily reached from **La Tour Fondue**, is the best one to visit—sandy beaches and fine views reward the visitor who wants peace and quiet.

The **Iles de Lérins** (the Ile Ste-Marguerite is the closer of the two to **Cannes**—the other is Ile St-Honorat) provide extensive views of the Côte d'Azur. Ste-Marguerite has a fortress to explore—St-Honorat a monastery; both are well wooded with pines and provide plenty of shady walking.

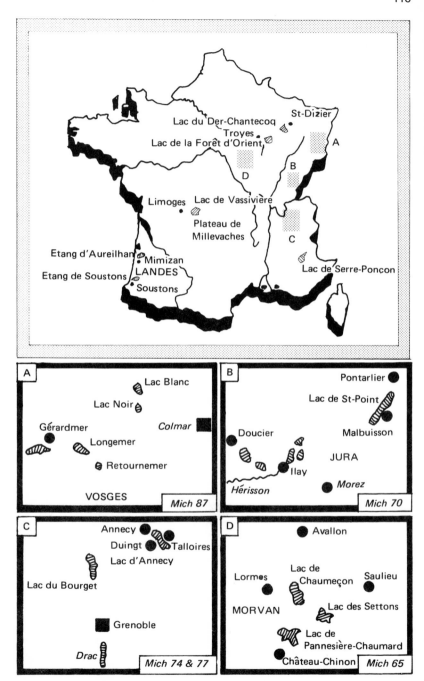

LAKES

Lakes return so many benefits to those who seek them out: scenic pleasures; fishing; boating; and swimming and other water sports are just a few of them. The lakes described here range from the smallest to the biggest in France: some are man-made —the others fashioned by Mother Nature, marvellously and alluringly.

The **Lac du Der-Chantecoq** is considered Europe's largest artificial lake—it is near **St-Dizier**; east of **Troyes** is the **Lac de la Forêt d'Orient**; both have large forests adjoining them and both are well equipped for water sports enthusiasts. The Forêt d'Orient is one of 20 French Regional Nature Parks.

At the other end of the scale, where will you find prettier stretches of water than the small lakes in the Vosges? My favourites are the lakes at **Gérardmer** and **Longemer**; but get out the magnifying glass and also find the tiny lake at **Retournemer** and the equally small **Lac Blanc** and **Lac Noir**—all three are lost amongst dark pine forests and are completely ignored by most tourists.

Deep in the heart of the Jura is **Lac de St-Point**, south of **Pontarlier** and close to the Swiss border. Attractive roads run down both sides of this narrow strip of water— **Malbuisson** is a pleasant centre. To the south-west are a handful of small lakes in the **Hérisson** Valley—the best are between **Ilay** and **Doucier**. The other attractions of these few kilometres are the two dozen or more cascades: the river falls over 250 metres in three kilometres and in wet weather the sight of the rushing water, shooting down the narrow valley, is a memorable one.

Further south still are the more famous, much larger lakes in Savoie. **Annecy** is a special favourite of mine. Drive right around the lake—the best views are from **Duingt**, across the lake from **Talloires**. But it is Talloires that is the sparkling *jewel* of **Lac d'Annecy**. No through road runs along the eastern shore and no trains are within miles; the absence of pollution and noise makes it a much nicer spot than most Swiss lakeside resorts. The lake yields *piscatorial treasures* unknown anywhere else in France. The menus of many restaurants in Annecy and the lakeside villages feature them: salmon trout; *omble chevalier*; *féra*; *lavaret*; *brochet*; and *lotte* (a burbot—not unlike an eel).

I have written elsewhere of **Lac du Bourget** but south of **Grenoble** is a man-made lake in the **Drac** Valley—at the northern end is the inevitable dam. Explore the eastern bank of this long, narrow strip of water; they have given it a name—the Corniche du Drac. Further south-east the first of the many dams built to harness the *white power* of the River Durance has created the **Lac de Serre-Ponçon**; some superb forests, new roads (use the D3) and mountains encircle it.

Within the boundaries of the **Morvan** Regional Nature Park are several lakes, unknown to the vast majority who ignore the hidden pleasures of Burgundy. The **Lac de Pannesière-Chaumard**, **Lac des Settons** and **Lac de Chaumeçon** have quiet roads circling them and are bordered by some of the finest small Burgundian towns: **Avallon**, **Lormes**, **Château-Chinon** and **Saulieu**.

East of **Limoges** is the man-made **Lac de Vassivière**. It lies on the edge of the strangely-named **Plateau de Millevaches**, near the point where no less than three of the finest French rivers spring to life: the Creuse; the Vienne; and the Vézère. The lake provides every type of water sport—in all directions are the gentle, quiet hills of Limousin. Few tourists make the detour to this quiet countryside.

Finally, I would like to draw your attention to a series of small lakes—*étangs* (ponds or pools)—in the pine forests of the **Landes**. They all add extra interest to the splendid beaches of the Atlantic coastline and the dense woodlands encircling them. Two are particularly quiet and interesting: **Etang de Soustons**—north of **Soustons**; and **Etang d'Aureilhan**—north of **Mimizan**.

Throughout France many lakes have *beach* facilities—ideal for swimming.

118

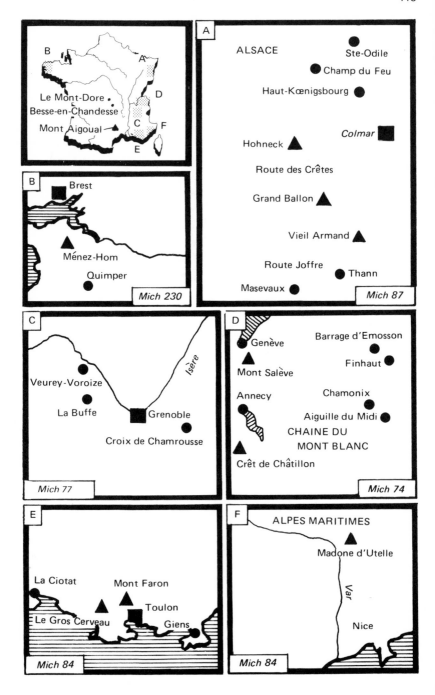

Many people get a very special satisfaction from going up mountains: serious climbers do it partly because of the competitive challenge it provides; the rest of us use much easier methods of getting to the top—but it is the thrill of the scenic views that attracts all of us up there.

My selection of mountain-top views all assume it will be a car that will get you to the viewpoint. Cable-cars take you to some of the greatest of all mountain summits—the **Aiguille du Midi**, towering above **Chamonix**, is the most famous example. But those trips cost money. If your holiday takes you close to any of the following don't miss them; it will be relatively cheap to make the ascent in your car.

Alsace provides the chance to set the scene for the pleasures that await this type of high-altitude scenic detour. Start at the ancient convent of **Ste-Odile** with its mysterious wall (none can guess its age). Now south-west to the **Champ du Feu**—then south-east to the castle at **Haut-Kœnigsbourg**; fine appetisers for the remaining run south along the **Route des Crêtes**. The **Hohneck** and **Grand Ballon** peaks are extra bonuses on this bracing mountain run. Stop at **Vieil Armand**—the view is marvellous, and you can also pay your respects at the National Cemetery, situated high above the Alsace Plain. If you have the time, finish the drive off with the short run from **Thann** to **Masevaux** (**Route Joffre**—D14).

South of **Genève** (Geneva), **Mont Salève** is an easy-to-make detour with extensive views. North of Chamonix (just inside the Swiss border) is the most spectacular of all the Alpine *free* views; a well-engineered road takes you from **Finhaut** up to the new **Barrage** (Dam) **d'Emosson**. On a clear day you will see both the Bernese Oberland peaks and the nearby **Chaîne du Mont Blanc**.

South of **Annecy**, to the west of the lake, is a narrow road that climbs up through dense forests to the **Crêt de Châtillon**. Choose a fine day and do the trip in late afternoon: I still remember vividly the astounding view of Mont Blanc.

Above **Grenoble** and to the east is the Chamrousse Massif. From the **Croix de Chamrousse** you win one of the most extensive panoramas in the Alps: mountains in all directions and far to the west even the Cévennes peaks are visible.

North-west of Grenoble is an *unknown* viewpoint: the climb to it—**La Buffe**—from **Veurey-Voroize** is a pretty one. From the entrance to the Tunnel du Mortier at its summit, you get an eagle's-eye view of the **Isère**, far below.

In the Massif Central, the observatory sitting on top of **Mont Aigoual** rewards any traveller's initiative in getting to it. The Aigoual is surrounded by the very best of the wild Cévennes country; full of natural curiosities, many of which are mentioned in the pages of this book.

In the northern half of the Massif Central lies the Auvergne: the best of all the mountain runs here is the D36 from **Besse-en-Chandesse** to **Le Mont-Dore**. It took me far too long to discover this short drive: don't make the same mistake.

In the south both **Nice** and **Toulon** have, on their northern doorsteps, some of the most interesting viewpoints in France. North of Nice, alongside the **Var**, is the high **Madone d'Utelle** peak with its splendid views of the **Alpes Maritimes**. Towering above Toulon are the twin viewpoints of **Le Gros Cerveau** (your view extends from **La Ciotat** in the west to **Giens** in the east) and **Mont Faron** (the harbour of Toulon sits below you—the view will please children especially).

I end with a simpler example in a region of France with no real mountains—Brittany. The **Ménez-Hom**, between **Brest** and **Quimper**, is no more than 330 metres high but the scenic aspects you enjoy from its summit are no less rewarding than from elsewhere in France. Here, there are all the pleasures of Brittany to fill your horizon: the sea; estuaries; and the gentle hills to the east.

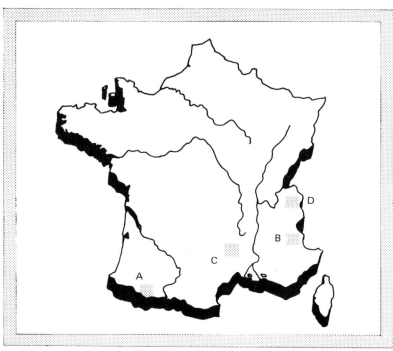

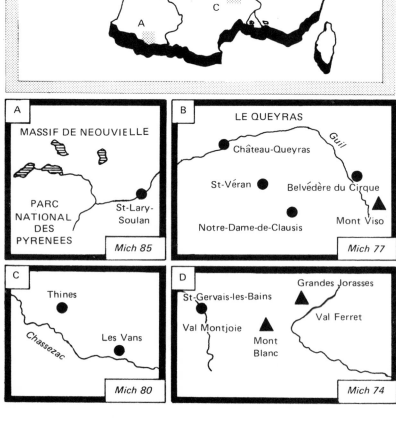

A

MASSIF DE NEOUVIELLE

PARC
NATIONAL
DES
PYRENEES

St-Lary-
Soulan

Mich 85

B

LE QUEYRAS

Château-Queyras

Guil

St-Véran

Belvédère du Cirque

Notre-Dame-de-Clausis

Mont Viso

Mich 77

C

Thines

Chassezac

Les Vans

Mich 80

D

St-Gervais-les-Bains

Grandes Jorasses

Val Montjoie

Val Ferret

Mont
Blanc

Mich 74

ROADS THAT GO NOWHERE

The loveliest parts of any country are frequently found by using *dead-end* roads—roads that, apparently, go nowhere. It was the organising of motor rallies 20 years ago that led me to discover some of the prettiest spots in Wales; access to many of them usually being from nothing more than farm tracks. The same advice applies to France—though I am not going to suggest you use farm tracks! My suggestions all use public highways, though many of them are narrow and are little-used roads; most of the year you will have them to yourself. I hope I will whet your appetite enough for you to make your own discoveries. All you need is the time and the right maps; as a result you will have a lot of fun and pleasure.

The most vivid examples of what I mean are found high in the Alps in the country called **Le Queyras**. Michelin map 77 is where you must diligently search—deep in the right hand bottom corner.

Two drives demand your attention. The first will take you from the imposing fortified castle, overlooking **Château-Queyras** (Hannibal is thought by many to have passed through here on his triumphant crossing of the Alps into Italy—one of the best strategic surprises in history), to **St-Véran**, the highest *commune* in Europe (2040 metres above sea-level). The population in the village has dwindled now to just a hundred or two and an economy of sorts keeps them living there; they grow crops, they keep cattle and they make furniture and wood carvings during the winter months. Skiing has brought winter rewards too!

Don't stop at St-Véran: continue up to the end of the road, to the chapel called **Notre-Dame-de-Clausis**, at a height of 2390 metres.

The second *dead-end* road lies to the east—the **Guil** Valley. Follow the river banks until the road stops you in your car tracks. You are within a short walk of the **Belvédère du Cirque**: superb views of **Mont Viso** (3841 metres) across the border into Italy, will be your just reward.

The Pyrénées provide me with a second chance to show you what the visitor can so easily miss: the **Massif de Néouvielle**. This is part of the **Parc National des Pyrénées**—sitting on the border with Spain. You approach this hidden mass of mountains and lakes from the D929, south-west of **St-Lary-Soulan**. Search it out on Michelin map 85—once more, in the bottom right hand corner. Woods, lakes, waterfalls, clear mountain air and countryside ignored by everyone else will be yours.

A third example is lost amongst the lonely, wooded hills north of the River **Chassezac**, west of **Les Vans** in the Massif Central. Seek out the village of **Thines**—an exceptional example of the secret Vivarais countryside. An attractive church and a pretty drive will ensure you don't regret the effort made.

Of the many other examples I could give you throughout France there are two I would specially draw your attention to—both of them in the Alps. The first is the **Val Montjoie** that runs south from **St-Gervais-les-Bains**; in the western shadow of **Mont Blanc** it rewards you well indeed. When the road stops, continue on foot, up the GR5: this is one of the most famous footpaths in France, stretching from Lake Geneva down to the Mediterranean. The second—and a real *must*—takes you through the Mont Blanc Tunnel into Italy. As you enter Italy turn east into the **Val Ferret**, a hidden, *dead-end* valley with spectacular views of the *other* side of Mont Blanc and the **Grandes Jorasses**. It is one of the best, unspoilt valleys in the Alps: once my wife and I spent a fascinating hour searching out the precise spot from where Whymper sketched one of his most famous engravings.

Get used to the idea of using narrow, *dead-end* roads whenever you can. You will really begin to think you have France to yourself. Inspiring views, ancient villages, rushing streams, extensive forests and solitude—you can want for nothing more.

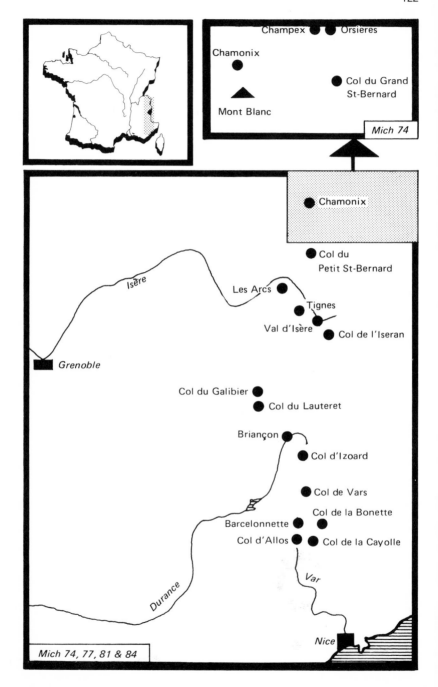

Champex Orsières

Chamonix

Col du Grand
St-Bernard

Mont Blanc

Mich 74

Chamonix

Col du
Petit St-Bernard

Isère

Les Arcs

Tignes

Val d'Isère Col de l'Iseran

Grenoble

Col du Galibier

Col du Lauteret

Briançon

Col d'Izoard

Col de Vars

Col de la Bonette

Barcelonnette

Col d'Allos Col de la Cayolle

Var

Durance

Nice

Mich 74, 77, 81 & 84

My insatiable passion for maps and motoring first took its grip in my teens; it will not surprise you to know that I was involved in motor rallying by the time I was 20! Combine these interests with a life-long love for mountains—I spent the first 10 years of my life in the high Himalayas—and the inevitable outcome found me, by 21, in the Alps, exploring all the high passes.

I have savoured the spell of these mountains at all seasons and at all times of the day and night! The suggested drive, at its best in early Autumn, is suitable for all of you: whatever your age. Provided you enjoy motoring and have a reliable, safe car, don't suffer from vertigo and have a sense of adventure—do it!

Start from the **Var** in the far south—as it turns 90-degrees to the west. I could suggest that you use either the **Col d'Allos** or the **Col de la Cayolle** as two alternative routes for the first hop to **Barcelonnette**. But I will plump for a third road—the newest and highest of the three: the mighty **Col de la Bonette**—2802 metres high. Your car will not take you anywhere higher in Europe. You could do all three! (One climb of the Allos was made in late spring when we must have been one of the first cars through after the long winter blockage: the hot sun in the brilliant, blue sky, the deep snow drifts, and the newly-opened alpine flowers, in the pastures where the snows had melted, were a delight—a combination of Nature's priceless gifts. We lingered far too long on the Allos that day.)

North from Barcelonnette is the steep **Col de Vars**, and hot on its tail comes the **Col d'Izoard**—2361 metres high. Both of these passes have their own *Refuge Napoléon*; erected on the orders of the great man in recognition of the enthusiastic welcome he received in the Alps on his return from Elba (see page 47).

Continuing north-west from **Briançon**, the countryside is dullish and you take two more high passes in rapid succession: the **Col du Lautaret** and the much higher **Col du Galibier**. Spare a thought for the Tour de France cyclists who regularly tackle these high passes during the hot month of July.

The next barrier is the **Col de l'Iseran** which, until the opening of the Bonette, was the highest of the Alpine passes. Glaciers and snowfields are to all sides throughout the summer; the road descends on the northern slopes to **Val d'Isère**, a leading winter sports resort. Other resorts are at **Tignes** and **Les Arcs**.

The last part of the route includes a detour via the **Col du Petit St-Bernard** into Italy. It is much the most scenic alternative as the views from the top of the pass looking north to the **Mont Blanc** Massif are spectacular indeed.

In the valley below you can do two things: either complete your journey to **Chamonix** by a short dash through the engineering marvel of the Mont Blanc Tunnel; alternatively, you can make a detour to the east across the **Col du Grand St-Bernard**. In the latter case don't use the tunnel; see the famous Hospice at the summit of the pass. The northern descent will give you an eye-opening demonstration of just what the Swiss can achieve with Alpine road engineering. At **Orsières**, make the short climb up to one of the most delightful small lakes in the entire Alps—at **Champex**; I predict you will want to stay there for a day or two!

Obviously this long drive can be made from north to south: my suggestion is better as the sun is always behind you—giving you much clearer views!

Two further suggestions: the entire route is full of opportunities to enjoy mountain picnics; in pastures alongside streams with scenic aspects to complement your food and water-cooled wine. When you stay overnight at any of the mountain towns—and provided it is a clear night—drive up to the summit of a local pass after your evening meal. The heavens seen at sea-level cannot compare with what you see from high altitude: don't miss the chance if you have it!

I hope it will not be too long before you enjoy this superb drive.

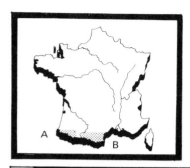

A

Pau

Mauléon-Licharre

Trois-Villes

Oloron-Ste-Marie

St-Gaudens

St-Jean-Pied-de-Port

Aramits

Lanne

Campan

Argelès-Gazost

Col d'Aubisque

St-Savin

Col d'Aspin

Laruns

Pic du Midi de Bigorre

Col du Tourmalet

Luz-St-Sauveur

Col de Peyresourde

Luchon

PYRENEES

Cirque de Gavarnie

Mich 85

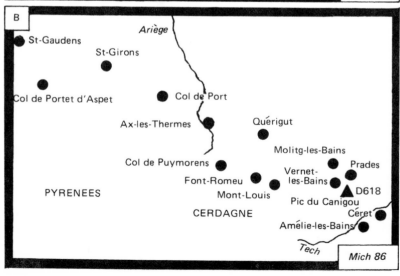

B

Ariège

St-Gaudens

St-Girons

Col de Portet d'Aspet

Col de Port

Ax-les-Thermes

Quérigut

Molitg-les-Bains

Col de Puymorens

Prades

Vernet-les-Bains

Font-Romeu

Mont-Louis

D618

PYRENEES

Pic du Canigou

Céret

CERDAGNE

Amélie-les-Bains

Tech

Mich 86

I have never had the same enthusiasm for the **Pyrénées** as I have had for the Alps. The Pyrénées have their own treasures—but, on the whole, they are stark mountains without the majestic grandeur of the Alps. I have never driven the various *Routes* during the course of one holiday; what I have seen are all the famous passes at different times over the years. Don't let my comments put you off—some parts of this run are very attractive indeed.

The Pyrénées are really two different ranges; south of **St-Gaudens** is where they form a natural split. A mass of peaks goes west to the Atlantic, and the second part of the range goes east to the Mediterranean. At each extremity of the ranges are people of two nationalities: to the west are the Basques; on the eastern seaboard are the present-day generations of Catalonia.

Start the trip at the small town of **St-Jean-Pied-de-Port**—a favourite of mine. **Mauléon-Licharre** is an old fortified stronghold and it marks the end of the Basque country and the beginning of the Béarn. Aramis of *The Three Musketeers* took his name from **Aramits**; **Lanne** (near Aramits) was the home of Monsieur de Porthau—who gave his name to Porthos; and the hamlet called **Trois-Villes**, 11 kilometres south of Mauléon, gave its name to Tréville.

Continue through **Oloron-Ste-Marie** and south to **Laruns**.

Here you start a magnificent series of high climbs. The first is the **Col d'Aubisque** —1709 metres high. The narrow road descending to the east deserves extra attention: it takes you down to the spa town of **Argelès-Gazost**. Don't use the main N21 that speeds you south: instead, make the short detour to **St-Savin**, a tiny village with a lovely Romanesque abbey.

You are close to the amazing **Cirque de Gavarnie**; don't miss it (page 103).

East from **Luz-St-Sauveur**, you climb again to an even higher pass—the **Col du Tourmalet**, 2115 metres above sea-level. If the toll road is open, make the ascent to the **Pic du Midi de Bigorre**—it provides spectacular views.

You descend into the **Campan** Valley—said to be the best in the whole range. Then continue south and east again via the **Col d'Aspin** (1489 metres) and the **Col de Peyresourde** (1569 metres) to **Luchon**—one of the most fashionable spas, amongst so many, in these mountains. The Aspin is a real delight—my favourite.

Remind yourself, as you traverse these passes, that the Tour de France cyclists climb and descend them all in a single day *stage*. How do they do it?

Gentler country and less demanding roads now lead east to **St-Girons**, via the **Col de Portet d'Aspet**. Continue south-east across the **Col de Port** to the **Ariège** Valley. From **Ax-les-Thermes** the traditional route takes you via the **Col de Puymorens** to the high verdant plateau of the **Cerdagne**. If you have the stomach for it, use the minor road climbing east from Ax, across to **Quérigut** (its ruined castle was built by the Cathars 700 years ago) and then drive south to the two differing high altitude resorts: **Mont-Louis**, an old town with fortifications designed by Vauban; and **Font-Romeu**, a new, modern place—regularly used by athletes for altitude training. The green plateau of the Cerdagne with dense forests to the north is an amazing contrast to the different country you will be seeing just 50 kilometres to the east. Savour it all before you head eastwards towards the coast.

All that remains is the descent to the Mediterranean. The delights of **Vernet-les-Bains** and **Prades** await you, and the huge **Pic du Canigou**, rising high to the south, is the last reminder of the stark Pyrénées. If time permits, detour to the green oasis of **Molitg-les-Bains** (north of Prades) and drive the narrow road numbered **D618** that takes you to the charming **Amélie-les-Bains** and **Céret**, both in the **Tech** Valley. Take your time as the road needs care.

BIENNE & AIN

This is the first of two opportunities I have given myself to persuade you to explore some of the unknown rivers of the **Jura**. This section is unusual in that it illustrates how two of the towns have prospered through manufacturing skills developed centuries ago—despite both of them being off the beaten track.

Start from **Arbois**; the town is famous for its rosé and sparkling white wine (*vin fou—mad* wine) and, of course, it's where Pasteur worked for so long. Nearby are several scenic gems—see pages 95 and 103. Detour via **Salins-les-Bains**, a spa town where salt has been mined since pre-Roman times. **Champagnole** is where you will see the **Ain** for the first time—its source is nearby, to the east.

Ignore the Ain for the moment and drive to **Morez**, on the **Bienne**. This town has prospered from the days—nearly 200 years ago—when it became famous for the making of spectacle frames. Follow the **Gorges de la Bienne** (D126) as closely as possible—eventually reaching **St-Claude**, a personal favourite of mine and much loved by Nevile Shute. The town tumbles down from the hills to the valley below; it is intriguing to realise—like Morez—that it prospered originally, 200 years ago, because of its reputation for making the world's best pipe briars.

Soon the Bienne joins the Ain. Detour north to see one example of the many man-made lakes, built in modern times to harness the power-creating waters of the Jura. Continue south following the narrow lanes alongside the Ain, until you reach **Poncin**. Drive a short distance east to **Cerdon**: nearby is an interesting cave, and high above the village is the memorial to those who died as members of the Resistance during the War—the *Maquis* of Ain. Finish your trip by exploring **Bourg-en-Bresse**. The **Eglise de Brou** and the adjoining Ain Museum (showing aspects of the Ain way of life over the centuries) are amongst its treasures. Enjoy the local *Vins du Bugey*—from the hills to the south-east.

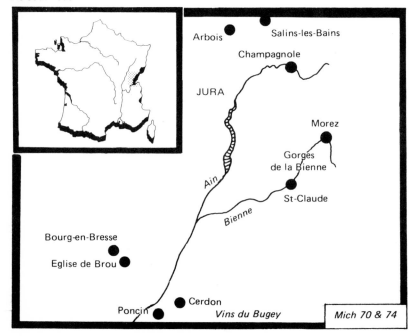

CHAPEAUROUX & ALLIER

My wife and I *discovered* the **Chapeauroux** by accident 20 years ago. We were on our way from **Mende** to **Le Puy** in our Mini with our young son aboard. The *obvious* route was via the **N88** through **Pradelles**. Neither my friends, nor my readers, will be surprised to hear that for me the *obvious* route had to be the wrong one. And, as I have discovered many times, my instinct proved me right!

So, it was up the **D988** we went chugging. What a delight that valley was in springtime. I cannot decide why (amongst tens of thousands of mental images I retain of past scenery, past roads and details from hundreds of maps) I can recall so vividly those few kilometres. Was it the sparkling April light, the rushing torrent—full of newly-melted clear water—or was it the emerging tints of spring? Whatever it was it remains brightly in my memory.

At the village of **Chapeauroux** we continued our *deviation*; along the eastern bank of the **Allier** we went—on the D40. Near **Prades** we called it a day.

Years later we returned to complete the Allier trip. From Prades we drove through **Chanteuges, Langeac, Aubazat, Lavoûte-Chilhac** and **Blassac**—all in the **Gorges de l'Allier**—finishing at **Brioude**. It is lovely country; full of picturesque villages, some with impressive sites and some with old churches.

All the countryside to both east and west of the young Allier deserves some of your valuable time. There are the obvious attractions of **Le Puy** (page 49) and the infant **Loire** (page 132) but, in addition, I would suggest you explore the terrain to the west of the Allier right across to the **N9**.

There is no better example in all France of just what dividends you reap when you get off the beaten track; the more you do so the more you enjoy yourself. This is countryside where a map will repay its small outlay a thousand times over; Michelin map 76 has rewarded my family with many happy days!

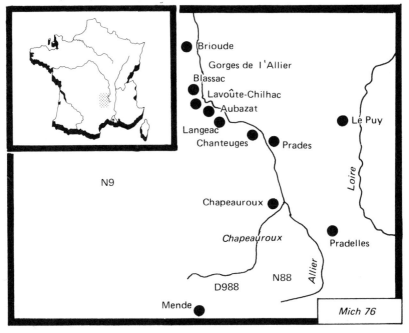

CHARENTONNE & RISLE

Elsewhere—*Detour in Normandy* see page 21—I set down some of the special delights that Normandy offers its visitors. Those delights are no less attractive in the unknown parts of these two river valleys.

The **Charentonne** is a tributary of the **Risle**. Start your northward drive at **St-Evroult-N.-D.-du-Bois**, near its source. It is a fine fishing stream and visitors making their way to its banks will be rewarded by solitude, the green pastures and woods, old villages and their ancient churches. Most of your early journey will be on the eastern banks—just before Bernay you will cross to the other side of the river. **Bernay** is endowed with many treasures—don't bypass them.

At the point where it joins up with the Risle, visit the chapel at **St-Eloi**. Use the west bank as you drive north to **Brionne**. There, cross the river to see the old ruined castle on the east bank. Then desert the river for a kilometre or two to find **Le Bec-Hellouin**—the abbey there played a tremendously important part in English history during the time of William the Conqueror (see page 51).

Now continue north again, using the west side of the river to **Pont-Audemer** which is full of timbered houses—the Auberge du Vieux Puits is a fine example.

Before you leave the area, make a short detour towards **Caudebec**. First enjoy the **Forêt de Brotonne** (a Regional Nature Park) and then cross the **Seine** by the new toll bridge at Caudebec. Make the short detour to the ancient Abbey of **St-Wandrille**, founded 1300 years ago. Complete your *deviation* by driving south, alongside the Seine, to the ancient Abbey of **Jumièges**; it is the most marvellous of ruins and it lies in a superb river setting. Main roads bypass it completely. Strange how it remains *hidden* to most tourists, unwilling to seek it out. That is true of so much of France—I do hope this book will contribute considerably to your enjoyment in encouraging you to explore the byways in the rural countryside.

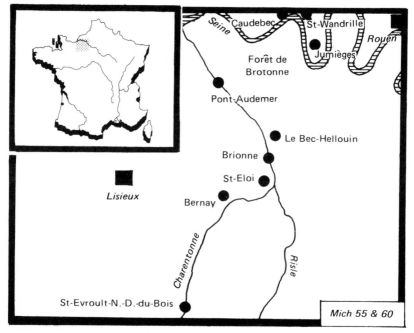

Mich 55 & 60

CURE & COUSIN

These two tiny rivers form an upside down V; there are many delightful diversions within the small swathe of emerald green country it encompasses.

Start at **Saulieu**, for long the gastronomic centre of Burgundy. It's an old town with narrow streets—walking is no hardship here. Drive slowly and carefully to the south-west, to the **Lac des Settons**—one of many lakes in the **Morvan** Regional Nature Park. Now continue north, choose any of the quiet road options open to you but be sure to see the waterfall at **Gouloux** (north-east of **Montsauche**). Carry on through **Dun-les-Places** and **Quarré-les-Tombes**. Explore the two forests to the east of the **Cure**—the **Forêt Chenue** and the **Forêt Au Duc**. Use the roads marked R.F. on the maps—one of these forest roads will take you to the natural attraction called **Rocher de la Pérouse**; you will see fine views to the south.

Now careful navigation is needed to get you to the **Barrage du Crescent**, at the northern end of another small, man-made lake. Within a kilometre or two is the Château of **Chastellux**—once the home of Colonel Labédoyère who, together with his entire regiment, came out of Grenoble to support Napoléon (see page 47).

The next stop must be **Pierre-Perthuis** with its old bridge over the Cure. Continue north to **St-Père** lying under the shadow of **Vézelay**, but with its own church—supposedly designed by St-Hugh, the architect of Lincoln Cathedral.

Turn east to the **Cousin** Valley. Explore the seven or eight kilometres stretch south of **Avallon**; walk as much of it as you can—it is exquisite. Finally soak up the atmosphere of Avallon itself, sitting high above the Cousin Valley. It is full of interesting churches, buildings, streets, ramparts, promenades and viewpoints. Joan of Arc, Napoléon, Mrs Simpson—all passed through this fine town. It was the birthplace of Vauban, the greatest of military architects—you will see his legacies to France throughout the country.

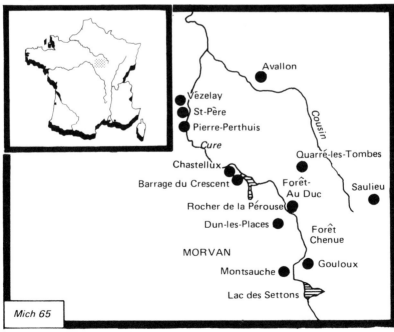

Mich 65

DESSOUBRE & DOUBS

Where, you might ask, is the **Dessoubre**? The map below makes it reasonably easy for you to pin it down. Make the detour to find it—I promise you will not regret the navigational effort needed to get there. The **Jura** is an area ignored by so many visitors to France—they miss a host of pleasures.

Start at its very source—or should I say—*above* it. The view from the **Roche du Prêtre** overlooks the magnificent **Cirque de Consolation**. Now descend down the narrow lanes to the valley-floor; a wonderland of springs, streams, trees and rocks. When you can bear to tear yourself away, drive the length of this stream to **St-Hippolyte**, where it joins the **Doubs**. Continue upstream alongside the Doubs, across the Swiss frontier to **St-Ursanne**. Cross the river and then climb the **Clos du Doubs**; to re-cross the river at **Soubey**. **Goumois** is your next destination. The river, the hills, the woods and the pastures are incomparable hereabouts: there is no greener, or lovelier part of France or Switzerland. I think it is at its best in autumn, when the lilac-shaded autumn crocus carpets the pastures.

Two marvellous natural sights have to be on your *must* list: the **Echelles de la Mort** and the **Saut du Doubs**. See the first—high above the wooded, narrow and rocky gorge—from a viewpoint, lost amongst the trees. Use the track off the **D292** at **Le Boulois** and walk the last few hundred metres—it's a spectacular scene. The astonishing cascade—the Saut du Doubs—is further upstream, part of the man-made **Lac de Chaillexon**—a short stretch of water but with several personalities!

Make a detour to the source of the **Loue**, north of **Pontarlier**; there's a great cavern where, at its mouth, a spectacular *show* of water cascades over rocks.

There is much more to see and enjoy upstream on the Doubs: there are the fine cheeses and wines from the Jura; marvellous forests; inexpensive hotels; seclusion and peace. What more can anyone want?

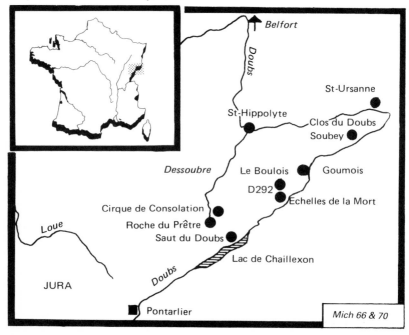

INDRE

Start your exploration of this river near its source—at **Châteaumeillant**. One good reason for giving you such sound advice is that it allows you to try its excellent VDQS red wines (made from the Gamay grape—the Beaujolais variety).

The first essential stop after Châteaumeillant is **La Châtre**, on a hill overlooking the **Indre**. This is the Vallée Noire (Black Valley) beloved by George Sand—visit the museum in the Rue Venose. Your next visit must be **Nohant**, six kilometres down the valley. Her home was here; a nostalgic, heart-stirring château full of memories of this legendary woman. Don't miss it.

Ardentes has a Romanesque church. The great oak **Forêt de Châteauroux** lies to the south of the town of that name and **Châteauroux** itself has several attractions.

Continue north-west to **Loches** with its famous Cité Médiévale (Medieval City). It's an imposing place, high above the town; with towers, a museum, keep and churches—it was built as a fortress. On the far side of the river are the ruins of the ancient abbey at **Beaulieu-lès-Loches**; further east, past fine forests, are the **Chartreuse du Liget** (built by Henry II as an act of repentance for the murder of Thomas à Becket) and pretty **Montrésor**, sitting alongside the **Indrois**.

Follow the **D10** and **D17** to **Montbazon**; you will miss a lot if you make the mistake of using the main N143 road. Beyond Montbazon is **Saché** where the château, surrounded by a park and woods, was for much of his life the home of Balzac—a museum at the château will interest you. Use the minor lanes alongside the river—all in fruit-growing country—to reach **Azay-le-Rideau** (see page 57).

Finally, just before the Indre flows into the **Loire**, spare some time for the château at **Ussé**. Cross the river by the bridge in front of it and admire this imposing structure, said to have inspired Perrault who used it as the setting for *Sleeping Beauty*; enjoy its flowered terraces, towers, turrets and woods.

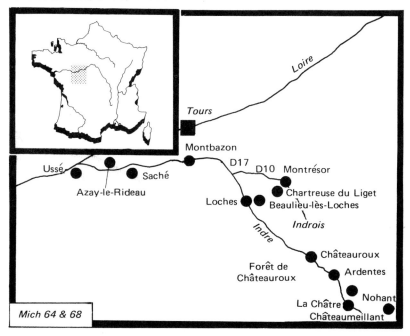

Mich 64 & 68

LOIRE

What, you ask, is this doing amongst the *Unknown Rivers of France*? The **Loire** (France's longest) is many rivers: lazy for most of its length, but it's a roaring torrent near its source, high in the Massif Central. We are going to explore the first few kilometres of its long journey to the Atlantic.

The first trickle emerges at the **Gerbier de Jonc**—high up in the **Ardèche**. Follow its banks to a man-made lake—which comes very early in its life—at **La Palisse**. Then part company with the river; no hardship this as the **Lac-d'Issarlès**, a kilometre or two to the north, is an attractive sight—an intense blue.

Navigate carefully to the next highlight; **Arlempdes**—on the west bank and further downstream. It has a really impressive site, château ruins and a tremendous view—all of which will make the effort to get there worthwhile. Then comes **Goudet** and, to the east, is **Le Monastier**, where Robert Louis Stevenson started his travels, in 1878, with Modestine (he bought the old animal here), later made famous in his book *Travels with a Donkey in the Cévennes*.

Rejoin the Loire east of **Le Puy**; passing through the **Gorges de Peyredeyre** where the river is a strong torrent. Near **Lavoûte-s-Loire** is the **Château Lavoûte-Polignac**. The château here has a remarkable and romantic site, sitting on a volcanic rock which falls vertically to the river below. This landscape was described by George Sand in 1859 as a *site grandoise*. Drive up any of the lanes to the west and enjoy the fine views of the countryside and river below you.

You can now choose between the various options open to you: to continue your journey down the Loire, enjoying many more of the gorges that the river has cut in its path down to **Roanne**; to go east into the pretty, wooded hills of the **Ardèche**; or to bear north-west into the volcanic hills and attractions of the **Auvergne**. How fortunate you will be to have such a difficult choice!

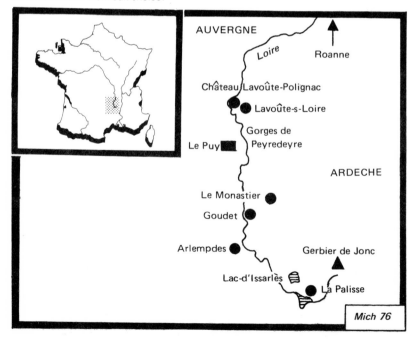

Mich 76

NIVE

This river runs through the countryside the French call *Pays Basque*.

Start your exploration in the foothills of the **Pyrénées**—near the frontier with Spain at **St-Jean-Pied-de-Port** (*port* means pass).

St-Jean-Pied-de-Port makes the ideal introduction to the pleasures of this corner of France. It was once an important stopping place for the pilgrims on their long road to St-Jacques-de-Compostelle (see page 49). La Ville Haute with its Citadel and ramparts sits high above the **Nive**, and down below, alongside the river, is the old town with its narrow streets, ancient houses and lovely bridge.

In my introduction I stress you make great use of the *Syndicat d'Initiative* (Tourist Office) in most French towns. Here, at St-Jean, is a perfect example. They will give you all the help and clues you need to get the best from the town and surrounding country. The various points that were so important to the pilgrims are all very clearly marked in the neighbourhood: look out for the *shell* sign of St-Jacques—the shell from *coquilles St-Jacques* (scallops).

Detour across the hills via **Irouléguy** (fine *local* wines are made here) to **St-Etienne-de-Baïgorry** on the **Nive des Aldudes**—tributary of the Nive. It is a gorgeous valley. We can remember one sparkling April day when it was difficult to tear ourselves away from the country south of St-Etienne (use **D948**).

But we did, to discover another delightful spot at **Cambo-les-Bains**; a mixture of a typical Basque village and a pleasant spa town. It is full of handsome trees; it is a great pity that the wise folk who planted them so long ago cannot now enjoy the splendid sight. The whole area is renowned for its mild winter climate.

Not far away are the caves called the **Grottes d'Oxocelhaya**. To the east of the river is the scenic **Route impériale des Cimes**. Whichever route you take, you are just kilometres away from the world famous resorts of **Biarritz** and **St-Jean-de-Luz**.

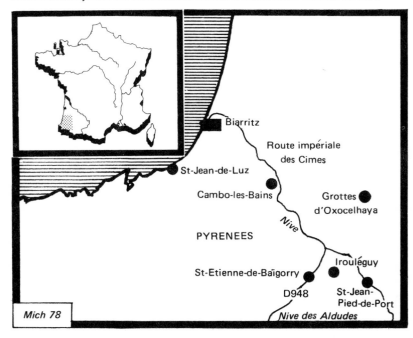

TRUYERE & LOT

Your starting point should be **St-Flour** (it has an unusual and impressive site—sitting as it does on top of its 100 metres high *table*), some 12 kilometres from the **Truyère**. Your first sighting of this river is a memorable one; seen from the N9 at the **Viaduc de Garabit**. This astonishing railway bridge was designed by Boyer and built by Eiffel, who conceived the Eiffel Tower in Paris.

The river has been made to *work* by the construction of a dam at **Grandval**. No roads line the banks of the man-made lake; nevertheless, the D13 is an exciting road that takes you through **Faverolles** and **Fridefont**—detour north to the splendid château ruins at **Alleuze**. Then on to **Chaudes-Aigues**—this place is unusual in that it gets its hot water from natural springs.

To the west the road descends to the river at **Pont de Tréboul**, where you cross a narrow man-made lake. Use the few lanes that do pass through the gorges though, at times, you can only use the roads to the north of the Truyère.

Several dams later you will arrive at **Entraygues** where a fine Gothic bridge graces this old pilgrimage stopping place. Make the short detour up the **Lot** to **Estaing** and **Espalion**; the Lot is at its best in this stretch. Estaing is dominated by its castle—Espalion by its 13th century bridge and castle. Enjoy the *local* wines hereabouts.

Retrace your steps downstream and follow the Lot. You should on no account miss the following: **Conques** (see page 49) will fascinate you; **St-Cirq-Lapopie**, clinging to the hillside, will enchant you; **Pech-Merle** and its underground treasures will thrill you; and your finishing point at **Cahors**—a charming town with a magnificent setting and its world-famous fortified bridge—will enthrall you.

But one final *detour* is the most exciting of all and it demonstrates vividly the value of maps. I implore you not to miss the fantastic castle at **Bonaguil**. It was considered impregnable when it was built—even today, it is easy to see why.

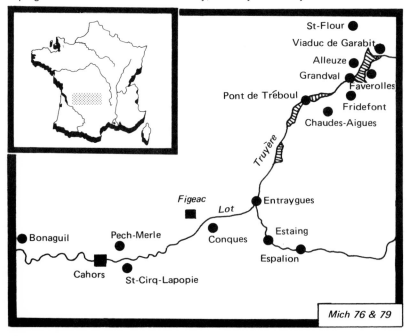

Mich 76 & 79

VEZERE

Enjoy this river—the most peaceful and serene of all rivers in the Dordogne region. Start at **Uzerche** on the N20: it is a fine small town, encircled by a loop of the river; there is no better setting to start any of my *Unknown Rivers of France* tours.

If time permits you may choose to explore the **Vézère** upstream to its source high in the strangely-named **Plateau de Millevaches**—a tableland of countless springs, where the Vienne, Creuse and other rivers all rise. Its name does not originate from *vaches* (cows) but from the old Celtic word *batz*—meaning spring. It is lonely, wild country—full of granite rocks and pine forests.

No roads follow the river banks for the first few kilometres downstream from Uzerche. Cross the river at **Vigeois** and travel the west bank towards **Orgnac**. Then make the exciting crossing of the river to **Estivaux**, on the east bank. Continue south to **Allassac**. Once there don't miss the short three kilometres run to the bridge at **Saillant**—a fine bridge complemented by charming river views.

Now you can follow the river banks. South of **Varetz**, on the west bank, is one of the finest châteaux hotels in France—the Castel Novel, on its own wooded hill. Guest or not, drive up through the woods and have a look at it! A few kilometres of dullish country follows—but things look up at **Montignac**. At nearby **Lascaux**, on September 12, 1940, four boys made the breathtaking discovery of prehistoric wall paintings of bison, deer and horses. Sadly, it is closed now, but at nearby **Les Eyzies** are several caves compensating for your disappointment.

The river is at its most charming between Montignac and the point at which it joins the **Dordogne**. All this is well-known country. So many jewels are close at hand: lovely **Sarlat**; **Beynac** and **La Roque-Gageac** (the two most picturesque of those *gems*); the hill towns of **Gourdon** and **Domme**; and the châteaux at **Fénelon** and **La Treyne**. Try to see all of them.

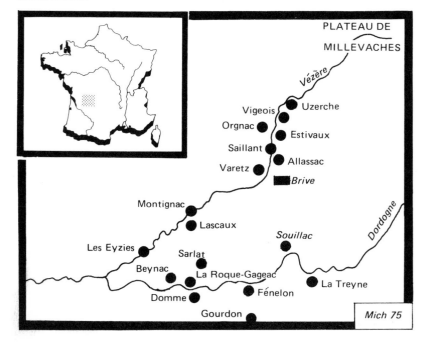

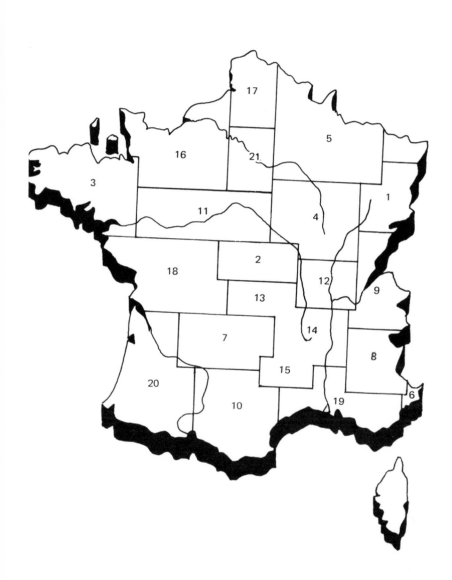

Use this regional index in addition to the general index of places: for example—if you are spending a few days in Burgundy the page numbers listed below for that region will refer you to the many chapters describing its myriad attractions. (The regions shown on the map facing this page, and listed below, correspond to those in **French Leave**—*simplifying the task of matching hotels and restaurants with the scenic pleasures of France.)*

1 **Alsace** 39, 61, 65, 67, 71, 75, 87, 89, 99, 117, 119, 130.

2 **Berry-Bourbonnais** 27, 49, 55, 87, 95, 101, 131.

3 **Brittany** 9, 13, 63, 65, 71, 75, 77, 79, 81, 83, 90, 91, 97, 99, 105, 115, 119.

4 **Burgundy** 11, 15, 39, 45, 47, 49, 53, 61, 65, 69, 75, 87, 91, 97, 117, 129.

5 **Champagne-Ardenne** 31, 41, 45, 53, 55, 61, 71, 75, 77, 87, 95, 97, 101, 117.

6 **Côte d'Azur** 25, 47, 59, 61, 63, 65, 67, 69, 75, 77, 79, 83, 85, 87, 99, 107, 109, 111, 115, 119, 123.

7 **Dordogne** 17, 23, 49, 55, 59, 61, 101, 113, 134, 135.

8 **Hautes-Alpes** 47, 59, 65, 67, 71, 75, 81, 85, 87, 89, 90, 95, 97, 99, 109, 113, 117, 119, 121, 123.

9 **Jura & Savoie** 53, 65, 67, 75, 81, 83, 85, 87, 89, 90, 95, 99, 101, 103, 111, 117, 119, 121, 123, 126, 130.

10 **Languedoc-Roussillon** 49, 53, 55, 59, 63, 65, 75, 77, 79, 91, 97, 99, 101, 103, 107, 111, 113, 125.

11 **Loire** 29, 45, 57, 67, 75, 87, 93, 131.

12 **Lyonnais** 11, 15, 39, 47, 53, 59, 65, 69, 75, 87, 93, 99, 111, 113, 126.

Massif Central:

   13 **Auvergne** 19, 23, 65, 83, 87, 89, 90, 97, 99, 101, 117, 119, 127.

   14 **Ardèche** 7, 19, 37, 65, 67, 85, 97, 101, 109, 132.

   15 **Cévennes** 103, 109, 111, 113, 119, 121, 127.

16 **Normandy** 21, 41, 45, 51, 55, 63, 65, 75, 79, 81, 83, 90, 95, 97, 99, 105, 128.

17 **North** 31, 41, 45, 55, 59, 63, 67, 69, 71, 77, 79, 83, 105.

18 **Poitou-Charentes** 33, 41, 45, 49, 53, 55, 63, 67, 69, 79, 93, 97, 101, 105, 115, 117.

19 **Provence** 35, 37, 59, 61, 63, 65, 67, 69, 75, 77, 79, 87, 89, 90, 93, 97, 99, 107, 109, 115, 119.

20 **Southwest** 39, 43, 49, 65, 67, 71, 79, 81, 83, 87, 89, 95, 97, 99, 101, 103, 105, 113, 117, 121, 125, 133.

21 **Ile de France** 43, 55, 61, 67, 73, 77, 95, 99.

Aa 41
Abîme du Bramabiau 113
Abîmes de la Fage 17
Agay 79
Agde 91
Agen 49, 91
Aiglun, Clue d' 25
Aigoual, Mont 113, 119
Aigues-Mortes 59, 93, 107
Aiguille, Mont 85
Aiguille du Midi 119
Ain 126
Ainay-le-Vieil 27
Aire-s-l'Adour 87
Aisne 31
Aix, Ile d' 33
Aix-en-Provence 35, 75, 77
Aix-les-Bains 87, 101
Albert 41, 67
Albi 55, 97
Alise-Sainte-Reine 11, 69
Allassac 135
Allègre 19
Alleuze 134
Allier 23
Allier, Gorges de l' 127
Allimas, Col de l' 85
Allos, Col d' 85, 123
L'Alpe-d'Huez 89
Alpes Maritimes 119
Alpilles, Chaîne des 35, 67, 69
Ambert 19, 90
Amboise 29
Amélie-les-Bains 101, 125
Amiens 31, 55
Ammerschwihr 39
Ancy-le-Franc 11
Les Andelys 21
Anet 73
Angers 57
Angles-s-l'Anglin 33, 93
Anglin 33, 93
Angoulême 33
Annay 11
Annecy 65, 81, 117, 119
Annecy, Lac d' 117
Annot 67, 87
Ansouis 35
Antibes 47, 77
Les Antiques 69
Antraigues 85
Apremont, Gorges d' 43
Apt 35, 69
Aquitaine 99
Aramits 125
Arbois 103, 126
Arcachon 99, 105
Les Arcs 123
Arcy, Grottes d' 11
Ardèche (River) 7
Ardèche, Gorges de l' 7
Ardèche, Vallée de l' 109
Ardentes 131
Ardusson 61
Argelès-Gazost 125
Argentat 17
Ariège 125
Arlempdes 132
Arles 49, 67, 69, 77
Armançon 11, 61
Armorique (Parc Régional) 13

Arrée, Monts d' 13
Arromanches 41
Arzal 91
Arzelier, Col de l' 85
Aspe, Gave d' 81
Aspin, Col d' 125
Aspres-s-Buëch 65
Au Duc, Forêt 129
Aubance 29
Aubazat 127
Aubazines 17
Aubenas 85
Aubisque, Col d' 125
Auch 49
Aude 59
Aude, Haute Vallée de l' 111
Aulnay 33, 49
Aulne 13, 81
Aups 109
Auray 9
Aurielhan, Etang d' 117
Auribeau 25
Aurillac 23
Authie 31
L'Aution 25
Autun 11, 15, 47, 53, 69, 97
Auxerre 15, 45, 47, 65, 75, 91
Auxey-Duresses 39
Avallon 11, 47, 53, 97, 117, 129
Avaloirs, Mont des 21
Aven 81
Aven Armand 113
Aven d'Orgnac 113
Avesnes 31
Avignon 75, 77, 90
Avoriaz 89
Avranches 21
Ax-les-Thermes 125
Aydat, Lac d' 23
Azay-le-Rideau 57, 131
Azé 11
Azincourt 41

Babaou, Col de 35
Bagnères-de-Luchon 89
Bagnoles-de-l'Orne 21
Bains-les-Bains 101
Balbigny 111
Ballon d'Alsace 89
La Balme-les-Grottes 113
Bandol 79, 115
Banyuls 107
Barbizon 43, 77, 95
Barbotan-les-Thermes 101
Barcelonnette 123
Barrage: see proper name
Bassac 33
La Baule 13, 79, 105
Baume, Cirque de 103
Les Baux-de-Provence 35, 61
Bayard, Col 47
Bayeux 21, 41, 51, 55, 105
Beaugency 45, 57
Beajolais 99
Beaulieu 107
Beaulieu-lès-Loches 131
Beaulieu-s-Dordogne 17
Beaumes-de-Venise 37
Beaumont-Hamel 41
Beaune 11, 39
Beauregard 29

Beauvais 55, 73
Beauvoir 27
Le Bec-Hellouin 51, 128
Belle-Ile 105, 115
Bellegarde 91
Belvédère du Cirque 121
Bendor, Ile de 115
Bénodet 9
Bénouville 41
Bergerac 17
Bernay 128
Besançon 75
Besbre 19, 27
Besse-en-Chandesse 119
Bétharram 113
Le Bettex 101
Beuvray, Mont 15
Beynac 61, 135
Bez 81
Béziers 91, 97, 113
Biarritz 79, 99, 101, 105, 133
Bienne 126
Bienne, Gorges de la 126
Biot 77
Le Blanc 33, 93
Blanc, Lac 117
Blanc, Mont 83, 101, 119, 121, 123
Blanc, Tunnel de Mont 121, 123
Blanc-Nez, Cap 105
Blanot 11
Blassac 127
Blavet 81
Bleine, Col de 25
Bléone 47
Blesle 101
Blois 57
Bois Chenu 45
Les Bois Noirs 19
Bonaguil 134
Bonette, Col de la 123
Bonnieux 35
Bordeaux 39, 65
Le Boréon 25
Bormes-les-Mimosas 35, 107
Bort, Barrage de 23
Bort-les-Orgues 23
Boscodon, Forêt de 95
Boucle du Hom 21
Boulogne 69, 71, 105
Le Boulois 130
Bourbon-l'Archambault 27, 101
La Bourboule 101
Bourcefranc 33
Bourdeilles 17
Bourg-en-Bresse 93, 126
Bourges 27, 49, 55
Bourget, Lac du 101, 117
Bourne 81
Bourne, Gorges de la 109
Brancion 15
Brantôme 17, 49
Bray-Dunes 105
Breil 65
Brest 13, 81, 115, 119
Briançon 59, 90 123
Brière 97
Le Brionnais 11
Brionne 81, 128
Brioude 101, 127
Brissac 29

Brive 17
Brotonne, Forêt de 128
Brotonne (Parc Régional) 97
Brou, Eglise de 126
Brouage 33
Brouilly, Mont 39
La Buffe 119
Buffon 11
Buis, Col de 85
Buron 23
Burzet 7, 19, 85
Busséol 23
Bussy-Rabutin 11
Butte de Montsec 97
Buxy 15

Cabrerets 113
Cabris 25
Cadenet 35
Caen 21, 41, 51
Cagnes-sur-Mer 77
Cahors 134
Calais 41, 45, 79, 105
Les Calanques 107
Calvados 81, 105
Camarat, Cap 107
Camargue 93, 97, 107
Cambo-les Bains 133
Cambrai 77
Campan 125
Canadel, Col du 35
Canaille, Cap 107
Cancale 9
Canche 31, 59
Canigou, Pic du 125
Cannes 25, 47, 79, 115
Cantal, Monts du 23
Cap: see proper name
Cap Roux, Pic du 25
Carcassonne 59, 97
La Cardinerie 41
Carnac 9
Carnelle, Forêt de 73
Caroux, Mont 97
Carteret 63
Cassis 63, 107
Castellane 47
Castelnau 17
Castres 49, 97
Le Cateau 77
Caudebec 21, 128
Caux 81, 105
Cayolle, Col de la 123
Cerdagne 65, 125
Cerdon 126
Cère 17
Céret 77, 125
Chaalis, Abbaye de 73
Chablis 11
Chagny 15
Chaillexon, Lac de 130
La Chaise-Dieu 19, 101
Chalon-s-Saône 47
Chalons 31
Chambéry 65
Chambolle-Musigny 39
Le Chambon 19
Chambon, Lac de 23, 93
Chambord 29, 57
Chamonix 83, 119, 123
Champagne 31

Champagnole 65, 95, 126
Champ du Feu 119
Champex 123
Chanteloup 29
Chanteuges 127
Chantilly 73
Chantilly, Forêt de 95
Chapeauroux 127
Chapeauroux (River) 127
Charentonne 128
La Charité-s-Loire 11, 49
Charlieu 11
Chartres 55, 73
Chartreuse 99, 111
Chartreuse du Liget 131
Chassezac 121
Chastellux 47, 129
Château: see proper name
Château-Chalon 103
Château-Chinon 15, 117
Château-Grillet 37
Châteaulin 81
Châteaumeillant 131
Châteauneuf 61
Châteauneuf-du-Faou 81
Châteauneuf-du-Pape 37
Château-Queyras 121
Châteauroux 131
Châteauroux, Forêt de 131
Châtelguyon 101
Châtellerault 33
Châtillon-en-Diois 81
Châtillon-sur-Chalaronne 93
La Châtre 49, 131
Chaudes-Aigues 101, 134
Chaumeçon, Lac de 117
Chaumont 11, 57
Chauvigny 33
Chavaniac-Lafayette 19
Chemilly 11
Chemin des Dames 31
Chénas 39
Chenavari 37
Chenonceaux 29, 57
Chenue, Forêt 129
Cher 27, 57, 93
Cherbourg 41, 65
Cheverny 57
Chinon 29, 45, 67
Chirols 7
Chitry 15
Cians, Gorges du 111
La Ciotat 119
Circuit (Auto) d'Auvergne 87
Cirque: see proper name
Citeaux 39, 53
Clairvaux 45, 53
Clamecy 15
Clamouse, Grotte de 113
Clermond-Ferrand 65, 87, 89, 101
Clos du Doubs 130
Cluny 11, 15, 53, 65
Cluses 90
Coaraze 25
Cognac 33
Cogolin 35
Col: see proper name
Collioure 35, 77, 79, 107
Collobrières 35
Collonges-la-Rouge 17

Colmar 39
Colombey-les-2-Eglises 45
Combe Laval 109
Combourg 9
Commarin 11
Commelles, Etangs de 73
Compiègne 45, 73, 87, 95
Comps 109
Comté 23
Concarneau 63
Condrieu 37
Conques 49, 134
Consolation, Cirque de 103, 130
Contes 25
Corbigny 15, 91
Cordès 23
Cormatin 11
Cornas 37
Corniche du Rhône 37
Corps 47, 71
Corrèze 17
Corsica 115
Cotentin 79
Cotignac 35, 99, 109
Coulanges 15
Coulon 93
Course 31
Cousin 129
Coutainville 105
Coutances 55
Crécy-en-Ponthieu 41
Crescent, Barrage de 129
Crêt de Châtillon 119
Crêt de l'Œillon 97
Creuse 33, 93
Croix de Bauzon, Col de la 85
Croix de Chamrousse 119
Croix Haute, Col de la 65
Le Crotoy 63, 105
Crozant 93
Le Crozet 19
Crozon 9
Cruas 37
Crussol, Château de 37
Cucheron, Col du 85
Cucuron 35
Culan 27
Cure 11, 129

Dampierre 73
Dargilan, Grotte de 113
Dax 101
Deauville 21, 79
Défile de Donzère 37
Demoiselles, Grotte des 113
Dentelles de Montmirail 37
Der-Chantecoq, Lac du 117
Des Gouttes 27
Dessoubre 130
Deux, Col des 85
Devèze, Grotte de la 113
La Devinière 29
Die 81, 87
Dieppe 63, 105
Digne 47, 65, 67
Dijon 11, 39, 61, 87
Dinan 9, 77
Dinard 9, 79, 83, 105
Dissay 33
Dives 51, 81
Divonne-les-Bains 83, 101

Dol-de-Bretagne 9
Les Dombes 93
Dôme, Puy de 89
Dômes, Monts 23
Domfront 21
Domme 61, 135
Dompierre 27, 67
Domrémy-la-Pucelle 45
Dordogne (River) 17, 23, 61, 135
Dore 19
Dore, Monts 23
Dormans 73
Dornecy 15
Douarnenez 9, 105
Douaumont, Fort de 41
Doubs 130
Doucier 117
Dourbie, Gorges de la 111
Doux 67
Drac 81, 117
Draguignan 77
Dreux 73
Drôme 81
Dronne 17
Duingt 117
Dunkerque (Dunkirk) 41
Dun-les-Places 129
Durance 35, 47, 59
Durdent 81
Durteint 61

Eawy, Forêt d' 95
Les Echelles 111
Echelles de la Mort 130
Ecouves, Forêt d' 21
Ecrins, Massif des 47
Eguisheim 39
Embrun 59, 95
Emosson, Barrage d' 119
Englancourt 31
Entraygues 134
Entrevaux 59, 85
Epernay 31
L'Epine 31
Epoisses 11
Ermenonville 73
Ermenonville, Forêt d' 95
L'Escarène 25
Escragnolles 47
Espalion 134
Estaing 134
Esterel, Massif de l' 25, 107
Estéron 25
Estivaux 67
Etang: see proper name
Etival 67
Etretat 83, 105
Eure 73
Evian-les-Bains 83, 101
Les Eyzies 113, 135

Falaise 41, 51
Faron, Mont 119
Faverolles 134
Fayolle, Col de la 85
Fécamp 105
Fédrun, Ile de 97
Félines, Col de 85
Fénelon 135
Fer à Cheval, Cirque du 103
Ferrat, Cap 107

Ferret, Val 121
La Ferté 73
Finhaut 119
Finistère 99
Foix 113
Le Folgoët 71
Fontainebleau 43, 73, 77, 95
Fontaine de Vaucluse 35
Fontenay 11, 53
Fontenay-le-Comte 33
Fontevraud 29
Fontfroide 53
Fontgombault 33, 53
Font-Romeu 125
Fontvieille 35, 67
Forêt: see proper name
Forêt d'Orient, Lac de la 117
Forez, Monts du 19
Fougères 13, 71
Fougères, Forêt de 13
Fougères-sur-Bièvre 29
Fouras 33
Franchard, Gorges de 43
Fréhel, Cap 9, 105
Fréjus 25, 69
Fridefont 134
Froissy 67
Fromentine 115

Galibier, Col du 123
Galamus, Gorges de 111
Gap 47
Garabit, Viaduc de 134
Garonne 39
Gartempe 33, 93
Gassin 35
Gavarnie, Cirque de 103, 125
Genève (Geneva) 65, 119
Gérardmer, Lac de 117
Gerbier de Jonc 7, 19, 132
Gevrey-Chambertin 39
Gien 45
Giens 119
Gigondas 37
Gimel-les-Cascades 17
Gironde 79, 105
Givet 31
Givry 15
Gordes 35, 77
Gorges: see proper name
Goudet 132
Gouffre d'Enfer 97
Gouffre de Padirac 113
Gouloux 129
Goumois 130
Gourdon 109, 135
Grand Ballon 119
Grand St-Bernard, Col du 123
Grand Brière 97
Grande Chartreuse 53
La Grande-Motte 79
Grandes Jorasses 121
Grands Goulets 109
Grandval 134
Grange de Meslay 29
Granier, Col du 85
Granville 63, 105
Grasse 25, 47, 77, 99
Grenoble 47, 65, 71, 75, 81, 85,
   89, 111, 113, 117, 119
Grimaud 35

Griz-Nez, Cap 105
Le Gros Cerveau 119
Grotte: see proper name
Guéhenno 13
Guerlédan, Lac de 13
Guiers Mort, Gorges du 111
Guiers Vif, Gorges du 111
Guil 121
Guimiliau 13

Halatte, Forêt d' 95
Hambye 21
Haras du Pin 21
Hary 31
Hautecombe 101
Hautefort 17
Haut-Kœnigsbourg 61, 119
Haut Languedoc (Parc Régional)
   97
Hautvillers 31
Le Havre 105
Helpe, Vallée de l' 31
Hennebont 9
Hérisson 117
Hohneck 119
Honfleur 63
Hospice de France 89
Huelgoat 13, 81, 90
Hyères 107
Hyères, Iles d' 115

If, Château d' 115
Ilay 117
Ile: see proper name
Ile de France 99
Indre 57, 131
Indrois 131
Irancy 15
Irouléguy 133
Iseran, Col de 123
Isère 67, 119
Isère, Val d' 123
Isle-Adam, Forêt de l' 73
L'Isle-s-Serein 11
Issarlès, Lac d' 132
Issoire 23
Izoard, Col d' 123

Jaligny 27
Joinville 45
Jonte, Gorges de la 111
Josselin 13
Joux, Forêt de la 95
Juan-les-Pins 47
Juliénas 39
Jullouville 105
Jumièges 51, 128
Jura 99, 103, 117

Kaysersberg 39
Kerjean 9

Labouiche 113
Labrède 39
Lac: see proper name
Lacaune, Monts de 97
Lacave 113
Laffrey 47
Lamastre 7, 67
Landes 67, 95, 97, 99, 105, 117
Langeac 127

Langeais 57
Languedoc 107
Lanne 125
Laon 31, 61, 71, 95
Lapalisse 19, 27
Laruns 125
Lascaux 113, 135
Lassay 21
Lassay-s-Croisne 29
Latour-de-Carol 65
Latronquière 17
La Latte 9
Lauteret, Col du 123
Lavaudieu 19
Le Lavandou 35, 79, 107
Lavoûte-Chilhac 127
Lavoûte-s-Loire 132
Lavoûte-Polignac, Château 132
Léman, Lac 101, 103
Lérins, Iles de 115
Libourne 39
Liesse 71
Liget 29
Lignières 27
Lignon 19
Limoges 117
Le Lioran 23
Lirac 37
Lisieux 81
Liverdun 97
Livradois, Monts du 23
Loches 45, 131
Locronan 9
Loing 77
Loir 29
Loire 7, 19, 29, 57, 79, 93, 105,
   111, 127, 132
Longemer, Lac de 117
Lormes 117
Lorraine (Parc Régional) 97
Lot 134
Loue 130
Loup, Gorges du 109
Lourdes 71, 103, 113
Lourmarin 35
Lubéron 35
Lubéron (Parc Régional) 97
Lucéram 25
Luchon 81
Le Lude 29
Lussac-les-Châteaux 33
Luxeuil-les-Bains 101
Luz-St-Sauveur 125
Lyon 39, 47, 65, 69, 75, 87, 93,
   113
Lyons-la-Forêt 95
Lys, Vallée du 89

Mâcon 11, 65
Madeleine, Monts de la 19
Madone d'Utelle 119
Magny-Cours 87
Maintenon 55, 73
Majeure, Vallée de l'Helpe 31
Malbuisson 117
Malestroit 13, 91
Malpasset 25
Mancelles, Alpes 21
Le Mans 87
Marais Poitevin 33, 93, 97
Marennes 33

Margaux 39
Marly 31
Marne 31, 73
Maroilles 31
Marquèze 67
Marsannay-la-Côte 39
Marseille 75, 107, 115
Masevaux 119
Massif: see proper name
Mauléon-Licharre 125
Maures, Massif des 35, 107
Maurs 17
Médavy, Château 21
Meillant 27
Melle 49
Melun 73
Mende 127
Ménez-Hom 119
Ménil-Glaise 21
Ménil-Hermei 21
Ménerbes 35
Menton 107
Mercurey 15
Mérigny 33
Meursault 39
Meuse 81
Meuse, Vallée de la 31
Meyrand, Col de 85
Meyrueis 113
Mézenc, Mont 7, 19
Midi, Canal du 91
Midi de Bigorre, Pic de 125
Millau 103, 109, 113
Mimizan 117
Moissac 91
Molitg-les-Bains 125
Monaco 25, 75, 107
Le Monastier 132
Monpazier 59
Mont: see proper name
Montagny 15
Montaigne 39
Montal 17
Montane 17
Montauban 91
Montbard 11
Montbazon 131
Montchanin (Le Creusot) 65
Montculot 11
Le Mont-Dore 101, 119
Monte-Carlo 25, 75, 87, 107
Montélimar 37
Monthermé 31
Montignac 135
Montjoie, Val 121
Mont-Louis 111, 125
Montmorillon 33
Montpellier 79, 99, 103, 113
Montpellier-le-Vieux 111
Montrésor 29, 131
Montreuil-sur-Mer 59
Mont-St-Michel 9, 105
Montsalvy 17
Montsauche 129
Morbihan, Golfe du 9
Moret 77
Morey-St-Denis 39
Morez 65, 126
Morlaix 9
Mortain 21, 41
Morvan (Parc Régional) 15, 97,

   117, 129
Morzine 89
Moselle 97
Mougins 83
Moulin, Château du 29
Le Moulinon 85
Moulins 27
Moulins de Paillas 35
Mourèze, Cirque de 103
Moustiers-Ste-Marie 99, 109
Mouton-Rothschild 39
Mulhouse 65, 87
Murat 23
La Mure 47, 67
Murol 23

Nancy 67
Nantes 13, 65, 75, 115
Nantes-Brest, Canal de 91
La Napoule 83
Narbonne 97
Navacelles, Cirque de 103
Navarrenx 81
Néouvieille, Massif de 121
Nevers 87
Nice 25, 65, 67, 75, 77, 107, 119
Le Nid d'Aigle 101
Nîmes 65, 69
Niort 33, 93
Nive 133
Nive des Aldudes 133
Nivernais, Canal du 91
Nogaro 87
Nogent-s-Seine 61
Nohant 131
Noir, Lac 117
Noires, Montagnes 13
Noirlac 27
Noirmoutier, Ile de 115
Normandie-Maine (Parc
   Régional) 97
Notre-Dame-de-Clausis 121
Nouaillé-Maupertuis 41
Noyers 11
Nuits-St-Georges 39

O, Château d' 21
Odet 9
Oise 31, 73
Oléron, Ile d' 67, 79, 115
Les Ollières-s-Eyrieux 85
Oloron, Gave d' 81
Oloron-Ste-Marie 81
Oppède-le-Vieux 35
Orange 7, 69
Orb 97
Orcival 23
Orgnac 135
Orléans 45
Orne 21, 81
Orsières 123
Ossau, Gave d' 81
Ossuaire de Douaumont 41
Ouche 11
Ouessant, Ile d' 115
Ours, Pic de l' 25
Oust 13
Oxocelhaya, Grottes d' 133

La Pacaudière 19
Paillon, Gorges du 25

Paimpol 9
Pal, Zoo du 27
La Palisse 132
Pannesière-Chaumard 15, 117
Le Paraclet 61
Paray-le-Monial 11
Paris 43, 47, 49, 61, 65, 73
Parthenay 33, 49
Patay 45
Pau 43, 83, 87, 99
Pauliac, Puy de 17
Pech-Merle, Grotte du 113, 134
Peille 25
Peillon 25
Peïra-Cava 25
Pendu, Col du 85
Périgueux 17, 49, 55
Pérouges 59
Perpignan 75, 99
Perros-Guirec 9, 105
Petit Rhône 93
Petit St-Bernard, Col du 123
Peyredeyre, Gorges de 132
Peyrehorade 81
Peyresourde, Col de 125
Pierrefonds 73, 95
Pierre-Gourde, Château de 37
Pierre-Perthuis 129
Pilat, Mont (Parc Régional) 97
Pique, Vallée de la 89
Pithiviers 67
Plateau de Millevaches 117, 135
Plats 37
Plombières 101
Plomion 31
Poilly 11
Point Sublime 109
Poitiers 33, 41, 45, 49, 53, 55, 93
Polignac 19
Pommard 39
Poncin 126
Pons 33, 49
Pont-Audemer 81, 128
Pont-Aven 63, 77
Pont-d'Ouilly 21
Pont de Tréboul 134
Le Pont-des-Vers 21
Pont du Gard 69
Pont-du-Loup 109
Pont-St-Esprit 109
Pontarlier 117, 130
Pontcharra 67
Pontivy 13
Pontmain 71
Porquerolles, Ile de 115
Port, Col de 125
Port-Barcarès 79
Port Cassafières 91
Port-Grimaud 35
Port-Leucate 79
Port Sud 91
Porte, Col de 85
Portet d'Aspet, Col de 125
Pouilly 61
Pourtalet, Col du 81
Pradelles 127
Prades 125, 127
Prenois 87
Prisces 31
Privas 85
Provins 61

Puget-Théniers 67
Putanges-Pont-Ecrepin 21
Puy: see proper name
Le Puy 19, 49, 127, 132
Puymorens, Col de 125
Pyrénées 49, 81, 89, 99, 103
Pyrénées (Parc National) 121

Quarré-les-Tombes 129
Quénécan, Forêt de 13
Quérigut 125
Queyras (Parc Régional) 97, 121
Quillan 111
Quimper 9, 119
Quimperlé 9

Rabodanges 21
Ramatuelle 35
Rambouillet 73
Rance 9
Ray-Pic, Cascade de 7, 19, 85
Raz, Pointe de 9
Ré, Ile de 79, 115
Reculée des Planches 103
Redon 13, 91
Reims 31, 45, 55
Renaison 19
Rennes 13
Retournemer, Lac de 117
Retz, Forêt de 95
Revard, Mont 87, 101
Rhône 7, 37, 97, 107
Rhône, Canal du 91
Rhue, Vallée de la 23
Ribeauvillé 39
Richelieu 29, 67
Riolan, Clue du 25
Riquewihr 39
Risle 81, 128
Rivau 29
River: see proper name
Roanne 41, 132
Robin, Mont 21
Roc Trévezel 13
Rocamadour 49, 113
Rochebonne, Château de 7
Roche du Prêtre 103, 130
Rochefort 33
La Rochelambert 19
La Rochelle 33, 63, 93, 105, 115
La Roche-Posay 33, 101
La Rochepot 15
Rocher de la Pérouse 127
La Rochette 67
Romorantin 29
La Roque-Gageac 61, 135
Rosanbo 9
Rouen 45, 75, 95, 99
Rousset, Col de 87
Roussillon 35, 69, 107
Route des Crêtes 23, 119
Route impériale des Cimes 133
Route Joffre 119
Rouvrou 21
Royan 79
Royat 83, 90, 99, 101
Royaumont, Abbaye de 73
Ru des Vaux de Cernay 73
Ruffaud, Etang de 17
Rully 15
Rumengol 71

Saâne 81
Les Sables-d'Olonne 79
Sabres 67
Saché 131
Saillant 135
St-Ambroise, Puy 27
St-Auban 25, 85
St-Bris 15
St-Cassien, Lac de 25
St-Céré 17
St-Cirq-Lapopie 134
St-Claude 65, 126
St-Cyprien 79
St-Die 67
St-Dizier 117
St-Eloi 128
St-Emilion 39
St-Etienne 97
St-Etienne-de-Baïgorry 133
St-Evroult-N.-D.-du-Bois 128
St-Florentin 65
St-Flour 134
St-Gaudens 125
St-Georges-de-Commiers 67
St-Germain-en-Laye 43, 73
St-Gervais-les-Bains 101, 121
St-Girons 125
St-Gobain 31
St-Gobain, Forêt de 95
St-Haon-le-Châtel 19
St-Hippolyte 130
St-Honorat, Ile 115
St-Honoré 15
St-Jean-d'Angély 49
St-Jean-de-Luz 79, 105, 133
St-Jean-Pied-de-Port 49, 125, 133
St-Lary-Soulan 121
St-Laurent-du-Pape 37
St-Laurent-du-Pont 111
St-Léger 15, 73
St-Lô 41
St-Malo 9, 13, 63, 79
St-Martin-du-Canigou 53
St-Martin-Vésubie 25
St-Michel, Montagne 13
St-Michel-les-Portes 85
St-Mihiel 97
St-Nazaire 13, 97
St-Nectaire 23, 101
St-Omer 31
St-Paul 61, 77
St-Paulien 19
St-Péray 37
St-Père 129
St-Pierre-de-Chartreuse 111
St-Pierre-d'Entremont 111
St-Point, Lac de 117
St-Pol-de-Léon 9
St-Pons 113
St-Pourçain-s-Sioule 27
St-Remy-de-Provence 35, 69
St-Riquier 31
St-Romain, Mont 15
St-Romain-de-Lerps 7, 37
St-Saturnin 23
St-Savin 33, 93
St-Sever, Forêt de 21
St-Thégonnec 13
St-Trojan 67
St-Tropez 35, 79, 107

St-Urbain 45
St-Ursanne 130
St-Valery-en-Caux 105
St-Vallier-de-Thiey 47
St-Véran 121
St-Wandrille 128
Ste-Agnès 25
Ste-Anne-d'Auray 71
Ste-Anne-la-Palud 71, 79
Ste-Baume, Massif de la 35
Ste-Catherine-de-Fierbois 45
Ste-Croix 21
Ste-Marguerite, Ile 115
Ste-Odile 119
Ste-Victoire, Montaigne 35, 77
Saintes 49, 69
Stes-Maries-de-la-Mer 93, 107
Salers 23
La Salette 47, 71
Salève, Mont 119
Salins-les-Bains 126
Samoëns 103
Samois 77
Sanary 115
Sancy, Puy de 23
Saône 15, 39
Sarlat 135
Sassenage 113
Saulieu 65, 117, 129
Saumur 57
Saut du Doubs 130
Sauveterre 81
Sédière 17
Seine 21, 43, 73, 77, 81, 105, 128
Semoy, Vallée de la 31
Semur-en-Auxois 11, 53, 61
Senlis 73, 95
Senones 67
Sens 75
Les Sept-Iles 105
Séranon 47
Serein 11
Serre-Ponçon, Lac de 117
Settons, Lac des 117, 129
Siagne 25
Sidobre 97
Silvacane 35
Sioule 27
Sioule, Gorges de la 27
Sisteron 47
Sizun, Cap 9, 105
Soissons 95
Sologne 93
Somme 31, 41, 67, 105
Soubey 130
Souillac 17
Sousceyrac 17
Soustons 117
Soustons, Etang de 117
Souvigny 27
Souville, Fort de 41
Spéracèdes 25
Strasbourg 65, 75
Suisse Normande 21
Sully 11, 125, 45
Superbagnères 89
Super Lioran 23

Tain-l'Hermitage 37
Taizé 15
Talcy 57
Talloires 117
Tanlay 11
Tannay 15
Tanneron 25
Tarn 111
Tarn, Gorges du 109, 113
Tavel 37
Tech 125
Tence 19, 97
Tende 65
La Terrasse 39
Thann 119
Thiepval 41
La Thiérache 31
Thiers 19
Thines 121
Thoissey 65
Thury-Harcourt 21, 90
Tignes 123
Tonnere 11
Touffou 33
Toul 97
Toulon 107, 119
Toulouse 49, 75, 91
Touques 81
Le Touquet 79, 83, 105
La Tour Fondue 115
Tourmalet, Col du 125
Tournon 37, 67
Tournus 11, 15
Tours 45, 75
Tourtour 35
Toury 27
Tramecourt 41
Trégastel-Plage 9
Tréguier 9
La Treyne 135
Les Trois-Epis 71
Trois-Villes 125
Tronçais, Forêt de 27, 95
Troumouse, Cirque de 103
Trouville 79
Troyes 117
Truyère 134
Tulle 17
La Turbie 107
Turenne 17
Turini, Col de 25

Ussé 131
Uzerche 135

Vaccarès, Etang de 93
Vacqueyras 37
Vaison-la-Romaine 37, 69
Val: see proper name
Val, Château du 23
Valbonne 83
Valençay 27
Valence 7, 65, 97
Valgaudemar 47
Vallauris 77
Vallée: see proper name
Vallon-Pont-d'Arc 109
Vals-les-Bains 7, 19, 85, 101

Vannes 9, 105
Les Vans 121
Var 25, 59, 85, 111, 119, 123
Varaville 51
Varengeville-s-Mer 105
Varetz 135
Vars, Col de 123
Vassivière, Lac de 117
Vaucouleurs 45
Vaux 15, 39
Vaux, Fort de 41
Vaux-le-Vicomte 73
Vence 61, 77, 109
Ventoux, Mont 37, 69, 87, 89
Vercors 81, 97, 99, 109
Verdon, Grand Canyon du 99, 109
Verdun 41, 97
Vernet-les-Bains 53, 99, 101, 125
Versailles 43, 73
Vervins 31
Verzy 31
Vésubie 25
Vésubie, Gorges de la 25
Veules-les-Roses 105
Veulettes-s-Mer 105
Veurey-Voroize 119
Vézelay 11, 49, 53, 129
Vézère 135
Vic-le-Comte 23
Vichy 101
Vieil Armand 119
Vienne (River) 33
Vienne 37
Vieux-Chambord 27
Vigeois 135
Vilaine 13, 91
Villandry 57
Villars-les-Dombes 93
Villecroze 109
Villefranche 63, 107
Villefranche-de-Conflent 65
Villeneuve-s-Yonne 91
Villeréal 59
Vis, Gorges de la 111
Viso, Mont 121
Vitré 13
Vittel 101
Vizille 47
Volcans d'Auvergne (Parc Régional) 97
Volnay 39
Vosges 99, 117
Vosne-Romanée 39
Vougeot 39
La Voulte-s-Rhône 37
Voulzie 61

Wimereux 79
Witzenheim 39

Yeu, Ile d' 115
Yères 81
Yonne 15
Yport 105
L'Yvette 73